EVERYONE A WINNER

Non-Competitive GAMES

FOR PEOPLE OF ALL AGES

Compiled by

Susan Butler

BETHANY HOUSE PUBLISHERS
MINNEAPOLIS, MINNESOTA 55438
A Division of Bethany Fellowship, Inc.

Copyright © 1986
Susan Butler
All Rights Reserved

Published by Bethany House Publishers
A Division of Bethany Fellowship, Inc.
6820 Auto Club Road, Minneapolis, Minnesota 55438

Printed in the United States of America

Library of Congress Cataloging-in-Publication Data

Butler, Susan.
    Non-competitive games for people of all ages.

    Includes index.
    1. Games. 2. Group games. I. Title.
GV1203.B83   1986   793   85-28644
ISBN 0-87123-812-8

THIS BOOK IS DEDICATED . . .
to all the members of The Work of Christ Community whose
faithful contributions of games, enthusiasm, and love have
made this book possible.

SUSAN BUTLER is a member of the Work of Christ Community in Lansing, Michigan. She was responsible for compiling and organizing the games.

In 1980, The Work of Christ Community assembled *Games*, compiled by Mary Hohenstein, a book of games which came from the many fellowship situations of the community. Because *Games* was so well received, *Noncompetitive Games* is being offered as a companion volume.

As in *Games*, most of the games in *Noncompetitive Games* have been enjoyed by various small groups within The Work of Christ Community. For instance, the Christian Childcare Center, a day care center/outreach of The Work of Christ Community, contributes games for preschool children.

Although this book presents strictly noncompetitive games, *Games* was not limited to competitive ones. Both books can be used as resources for the no-losers games style.

TABLE OF CONTENTS

MIXERS AND FIRST-MEETING GAMES

CIRCLE AND PASS-IT-ON GAMES

GUESSING GAMES

WORD GAMES

CREATIVE GAMES

DRAMATIC GAMES

RHYTHM AND MUSIC GAMES

STORYTELLING GAMES

RELATIONSHIP-BUILDING GAMES

ACTIVE GAMES

INTRODUCTION

As work began on *Noncompetitive Games for People of All Ages*, a friend of mine objected that there was no such thing as a noncompetitive game. If you don't compete, it's not a game, he claimed. He raised a good question.

If you don't win or lose, what makes it a game?

Challenge. Striving for greater achievement, individually or as a group, is rewarding, and it can be done without creating winners and losers.

Laughter. While trying to achieve a goal, fun is a by-product, often more valuable than the goal itself.

Development. Another by-product of a group-achieved goal is increased knowledge of our world, ourselves and each other. Physical, psychological, social, and spiritual growth are fostered.

What is the advantage of a noncompetitive game?

When everyone is dead set on winning, sometimes relationships suffer. The less talented end up losing often, and their self-esteem flags. New people may feel pressured and withdraw.

Noncompetitive games set people at ease. Cooperation flourishes, and everyone feels successful.

Of course, competitive games have a place as well. The game leader should consider the needs of his group when selecting activities.

How do you select a noncompetitive game?

The heading of each game helps you to determine whether

11

it meets the needs of your particular group. (See How to Use *Noncompetitive Games*.)

Two categories of children's games are identified. The other games are appropriate for older children and adults. However, these divisions should not be taken too strictly. Many games can be scaled up or down, depending on the age of the players.

A Word of Caution:

Almost any game can be played competitively or noncompetitively, depending on the spirit with which it is approached. A sensitive game leader will prepare his group by explaining the purpose of a game before they begin playing.

HOW TO USE
NONCOMPETITIVE GAMES

The format of *Noncompetitive Games* is intended to help the leader identify games most appropriate for his group. The introduction to each game explains the application of those games, and also suggests other games found throughout the book. The headings below the game titles help the reader compare each game with his specific needs:

Number of People: 4–10

Means at least 4 players are needed. More than 10 would be impractical. Usually the ideal number lies somewhere in between.

Length of Time: 10–60 minutes

Means a small group could play the game long enough to enjoy it or complete it once in 10 minutes. The longest any group would probably want to continue would be 60 minutes.

Materials: Paper and pencils

Means paper and pencils are needed to prepare for or to play the game.

Playing Site: Outdoors

Usually this is listed only if a location other than a typical indoor setting is needed.

Preparation: The materials are hidden from sight.

Refers to anything that must be accomplished ahead of time. "Preparation" does not include actions performed by the players as they begin to play the game.

13

Object of the Game: To write the other players' names.

Refers to the specific task to be performed. Usually more will be accomplished in playing the game than the simple "object." The overall benefit is often explained under "Comments," or in the introduction to the game category.

To Play: The group gathers in a circle and . . .

Means what the group needs to do to play the game.

Variations: For an additional challenge, names are written upside down.

Suggests ways to change the game for different age groups or simply for variety.

Comments: The players learn the names of new people.

Helpful tips or insights are communicated.

GAMES FOR PRESCHOOL CHILDREN

Small children will enjoy recognizing familiar objects and telling what they know in *Games for the Mind and Senses*. They will also be sharpening their skills of observation and memory. The *More Active Games* described provide the thrill of suspense without the agony of defeat.

See Also:

Games for School-Age Children
People-to-People
Songs Illustrated
Active Games

Games for the Mind and Senses

Look and See

Number of Players: Up to 8

Length of Time: 5–15 minutes

Materials: Several small objects

Object of the Game: To identify the missing object.

To Play:

The objects are placed on a table in front of the children. The leader draws the children's attention to each object and identifies it. While the children close their eyes, the leader removes one of the objects. After they open their eyes, the children are called upon to identify the missing object by observing the ones that remain. The game can be repeated many times.

Variations:

There are several ways to increase the level of difficulty:
1. The objects are in full view, but the leader does not draw special attention to them.
2. A greater number of objects are used.
3. More than one object is removed each time.
4. The time allowed for observation before eyes are closed is shortened.
5. While eyes are closed, the leader moves the objects around, so their positions no longer support the players' memories.
6. Instead of using objects on a table, the leader designates a child to leave the room, and the others then identify who is missing. This version could be played with a larger group.

Comment:

"Look and See" is also appropriate for older children and adults if a higher level of difficulty is employed.

Listening Test

Number of Players: Up to 8

Length of Time: 5–10 minutes

Materials: Things that make familiar noises, a screen large enough to obscure the noisemakers

Preparation: The materials are hidden behind the screen.

Object of the Game: To identify the sounds produced.

To Play:

The children listen to sounds produced behind the screen and identify them either by turn or spontaneously. The sounds may be musical instruments, familiar toys, dripping water, etc.

Variation:

A record with sound effects is played.

Smell Test

Number of Players: Up to 8

Length of Time: 5–10 minutes

Materials: Common objects or materials that have a distinct scent, blindfolds (optional)

Object of the Game: To identify things by smelling them.

To Play:

As the children close their eyes or are blindfolded, they each take a turn smelling an object and identifying it. The objects should be easily recognizable to the children, e.g., bubble gum, a flower, peanut butter.

Comment:

The leader should be sure no harmful materials are used, e.g., paints, solvents, glues, etc.

Games for the Mind and Senses

Reach and Feel

Number of Players: Up to 8

Length of Time: 5–10 minutes

Materials: Bag or box, objects children can identify by feel

Preparation: Objects are placed in the bag or box.

Object of the Game: To identify objects by feeling them.

To Play:

The children take turns reaching into the bag, without looking into it, feeling an object, and announcing what it is. Each child takes out the object he identifies before the next child takes a turn.

Variations:

1. "Reach and Feel" can be made easier or more difficult to meet the needs of the group by varying the particular objects used.
2. For younger children, the objects may be placed in view before they are placed in the bag.

Games for the Mind and Senses

Guess Who

Number of Players: 5–10

Length of Time: 5–10 minutes

Object of the Game: To identify the child described.

To Play:

The leader says, "I see someone who . . ." and describes a child in the group, e.g., ". . . is wearing a red ribbon." The child described can reveal himself, or the other children can look for him and say his name. If one distinguishing trait cannot be easily seen, two can be mentioned that make him unique, e.g., ". . . has brown hair and a striped T-shirt." Usually the game continues until all the children have been identified.

Games for the Mind and Senses

Following Directions

Number of Players: Up to 8

Length of Time: 10–20 minutes

Object of the Game: To listen carefully to the directions and follow them exactly.

To Play:

The leader calls on a child and gives him a set of directions, e.g., "Stand up, walk to the door, and knock on it." The child must listen carefully and follow the directions exactly. The next child is given a new set of directions. The game continues until all have participated.

Variations:

1. "Following Directions" can be easily suited to any age group by making the directions simpler or more complicated. This makes the game ideal for a group of widely varying ages.
2. "Following Directions" can be made more demanding by calling the child's name *after* the directions are given. The children will then have to pay close attention every time.

Comments:

Although it sounds simple, young children take this game as a great challenge. They will be encouraged if their performances are responded to with applause and cheers from the group.

Games for the Mind and Senses

What Comes Next?

Number of Players: Up to 30

Length of Time: 5–20 minutes

Material: Story familiar to the group

Object of the Game: To remember parts of a familiar story.

To Play:

The leader reads a story that the children know, pausing periodically to let the children finish a sentence or supply a word. The children enjoy the satisfaction of remembering the story.

Continuous Hot Potato

Number of Players: 3–30

Length of Time: 5–15 minutes

Materials: Ball made of soft cloth, music source
                          (such as a record or piano)

Object of the Game: To pass the ball before the music stops.

To Play:

The children sit in a circle and pass the ball (which they are told is a very hot potato) as quickly as possible, until the music stops. When the music is interrupted, the child holding the hot potato throws or rolls it across the circle, because it is too hot to handle. No one is eliminated. Instead, when the music resumes, a child near the ball merely picks it up and continues the game.

Comment:

Children like the excitement of pretending the ball is hot, and enjoy the game more without the disappointment of being "out."

Nonelimination Musical Chairs

Number of Players: Up to 12

Length of Time: 5–15 minutes

Materials: A chair for every player, a record and record player, musical instrument, or singer

Preparation: The chairs are arranged in a random cluster.

Object of the Game: To be seated as quickly as possible when the music stops.

To Play:

While music is played or sung, the children walk around the chairs. When the leader stops the music, the children must each find a chair and sit in it as quickly as possible. Even though there is a chair available for each child, for young children, this is sufficiently challenging. The game can be repeated several times with the same procedure, or followed by the variations below.

Variations:

1. The chairs are scattered around the room instead of in a cluster. This increases the level of activity.
2. A chair is removed after each round. The goal is for all the children to be seated somehow—on laps, if necessary. The children try to play as many rounds as possible, fitting everyone somewhere on the pile.

3. Musical Colors: Instead of chairs, colored squares of paper are placed on the floor. When the music stops, everyone must have at least one foot on a square. The squares are removed, one by one, until the whole group is sharing one or two squares.

Feather Blow

Number of Players: Up to 20

Length of Time: 5–15 minutes

Materials: A feather for each child

Playing site: Large open area

Object of the Game: To keep a feather off the ground.

To Play:

Each child is given a feather, which he tries to keep in the air as long as possible without touching it—in other words, by blowing underneath it. Of course, if it does fall, he may pick it up and try again.

Variation:

Each child is given a balloon to keep aloft by tapping it with his hands.

Caterpillar Over the Mountain

Number of Players: 4–20

Length of Time: 10–30 minutes

Materials: Bench(es) and tumbling mat(s) or similar materials

Preparation: A mountain can be constructed by an adult, or children may enjoy assisting. A mountain or a range of mountains are set up by placing the tumbling mats over the benches to form a path from the floor over each bench.

Object of the Game: To crawl around the room in the form of a giant caterpillar.

To Play:

Four or more children compose each caterpillar by walking on hands and knees, each holding the ankles of the child in front of him. The caterpillars walk around the room a little bit, then climb a mountain and slide down the other side. The caterpillars may begin small, then link up to form one long creature. Background music may add to the fun.

GAMES FOR SCHOOL-AGE CHILDREN

These games range from the quiet artistry of "Picture Letters" to the pandemonium of "Jungle Din." In some games children may need guidance to channel their activity into team work.

See Also:

Games for Preschool Children
People-to-People
Circle and Pass-It-On Games
Daffy Definitions
Finish the Mystery
Machine Charades
Clap-a-Rhythm
Don't Look
Quick-Change Artists
Describo
Encrypted Messages
Songs Illustrated
Greasy Spoon
Dramatic Games
Rhythm and Music Games
Continuous Story
Novel Objects
Reminiscing
Personal Photographs
Yarn Circle
A Different Door Prize
Active Games
Water Games
Stunts
Travel Games

I Made A Tasty Cake

Number of Players: 1–30

Length of Time: 10–30 minutes

Materials: Chalk and chalkboard or paper and pencil (Optional: Guitar or piano)

Object of the Game: To write a song as a group.

To Play:

The leader sings "I Made a Tasty Cake" (below) to the tune of "The Farmer in the Dell."

> I made a tasty <u>cake,</u>
> <u>Out of a rattlesnake.</u>
> And, do you know?
> <u>I loved it so!</u>
> I made a tasty <u>cake.</u>

The leader then asks the children for their own words to substitute for the ones underlined above. He may sing the verse below for another example.

> I made a tasty <u>pie,</u>
> <u>Eleven stories high.</u>
> And do you know?
> <u>It made me grow!</u>
> I made a tasty <u>pie.</u>

The leader writes down the new words suggested by the children, and then they all sing the new song they have written.

Comments:

Children ages 7–11 will enjoy this game the most because they love to rhyme. They will also be developing their language and creativity skills.

My Ship Has Come In

Number of Players: 3–20

Length of Time: 10–30 minutes

Object of the Game: To imitate a favorite toy.

To Play:

Each child takes a turn saying, "My ship has come in, bring-ing a _____," supplying the name of the toy of his choice. The child then imitates the toy mentioned. This will stimu-late the imagination.

Variation:

A little wilder, but just as much fun: As the child begins to imitate his toy, the other children join him.

Picture Letters

Number of Players: 1–50

Length of Time: 10–30 minutes

Materials: Chalk, chalkboard, paper and crayons
                         for each child

Object of the Game: To create a picture using a letter of the
                         alphabet.

To Play:

The leader writes a letter on the board for the children to copy. Each child then makes a picture using the letter as a starting point. It may be helpful for the leader to give examples, using other letters. The children may then share their creations with one another.

Variations:

1. Numerals are used rather than letters.
2. Older children may enjoy using more than one letter at a time, even short words as skeletons for their pictures.

Moderately Active Games

Anatomy

Number of Players: 2–20

Length of Time: 10–45 minutes

Object of the Game: To guess the body part selected.

To Play:

The children sit in a circle, with one child in the center. While the child in the center closes his eyes, one of the others points to a body part to be guessed. The child in the center then opens his eyes and calls on the others to give clues to help him guess the body part selected. If the part was a finger, clues might be, "Some people put jewelry on it," and "You might need it to do arithmetic." When the child in the middle guesses the part, the child who gave him the last clue sits in the middle, although this might be modified to give everyone a turn.

Comments:

This game should be supervised by an adult. If necessary, children can be instructed to look to the supervisor for a "good-choice" nod of the head.

Story Stretch

Number of Players: Any

Length of Time: 5–15 minutes

Preparation: The leader may prepare a story, or may improvise as he tells it.

Object of the Game: To listen to and act out a story.

To Play:

The leader tells a story, pausing every sentence or two to dramatize part of it for the children to imitate. The motions might include getting out of bed, dressing, eating, going on some adventure, and eventually arriving back home.

Comment:

Besides the enjoyment of participating in a story, "Story Stretch" allows children to release their wiggles and be ready for the next activity.

Flying Blind

Number of Players: 3–20

Length of Time: 10–45 minutes

Material: Blindfold

Object of the Game: To find a designated object.

To Play:

One at a time, each child is blindfolded, spun around, and instructed to find a familiar object in the room.

Variation:

After the child is blindfolded, a piece or two of furniture is moved to further confusion.

Statues

Number of Players: 2–10

Length of Time: 15–60 minutes

Playing Site: Outdoors

Object of the Game: To identify each statue.

To Play:

A child appointed as the sculptor takes each of the other children by the hand, swings them around, and releases them, so that they are flung staggering away, sometimes falling to the ground. As they land, each child freezes in any position he wishes, to represent a famous person, animal, or other creature. When all the "statues" are erected, the sculptor asks each one what he is, using yes-or-no questions, until he has identified them all. The game can then be repeated with a new sculptor.

Variations:

1. The statues are limited to a category such as animals, Bible characters, etc.
2. The statues are allowed to speak or make noises that give hints to the sculptor.

Comment:

"Statues" can be an educational game for children learning about Bible characters or historical figures.

Sock-Off

Number of Players: 4–12

Length of Time: 5–10 minutes

Materials: A pair of socks for each player

Preparation: Each player wears socks, but no shoes.

Object of the Game: To remove the socks from the other players.

To Play:

At a "go" signal, the players begin removing each other's socks as quickly as possible. The result is a mad scramble which is as much fun to watch as it is to play. If a more tangible goal is desired, the group can try to improve on the time taken to remove all the socks.

Variation:

All socks are removed. The players put them on each other instead of taking them off. They might also try to give each player a matching pair.

Comment:

"Sock-Off" is especially suitable for young boys.

One-of-Each Piñata

Number of Players: 3–25

Length of Time: 10–30 minutes

Materials: Piñata, blindfold, candy, small toys and stick.

Playing Site: Large room free of breakable objects, or outdoors

Preparation: A variety of candies and small toys are collected so that there is at least one of each for every child. The piñata is filled with the goodies and suspended above the children's heads with a rope, in such a way that an adult leader can pull it up and down.

Object of the Game: To collect one of each kind of candy and toy that falls from the piñata.

To Play:

One by one the children are blindfolded and spun around, and given a chance to strike the piñata with a stick. An adult pulls on the rope to move the piñata up or down at his discretion. When the piñata finally breaks and pours forth its treasure, the children try to collect one and only one of each toy, candy, etc. An adult inspects each child's catch to make sure each child has one of everything, and to make sure no one got carried away and grabbed too much.

Comments:

By collecting only one of each treat, the mob-rule element of

Very Active Games

piñata is prevented, and children have the challenge of trying to locate all the varieties. Filling the piñata with small toys as well as candies adds variety and cuts down on the children's sugar consumption. If small rubber balls are included, they will bounce in all directions when they hit the floor, adding to the excitement.

Jungle Din

Number of Players: 6–50

Length of Time: 15–30 minutes

Materials: Candy and paper bags

Playing site: Large open area

Preparation: Bunches of candy are concealed throughout the playing area.

Object of the Game: To find and collect the candy.

To Play:

The group is divided into packs of wild animals and a captain is appointed for each pack. Since each pack is composed of a different species, each has a unique call, which its members practice before proceeding. When a signal is given to begin, all the animals are free to roam the area in search of food. When any animal finds a cache of candy, he makes his pack call, which is the signal for his pack captain to come and retrieve the candy, storing it in a paper bag. Only the captains may collect the candy. When all the candy has been discovered, the animals meet by pack to enjoy their candy.

Variations:

Instead of simply dividing the players into packs, each player is secretly told the name of his animal. The animals then wander around, making cries appropriate to their animal identities, until they have found their fellow pack members. The game then proceeds as described above.

Hunting Games

Comment:

If, at the end of the candy search, some packs obviously have more candy than others, they should share some of it with the other packs.

Hidden Treasure

Number of Players: 4–30

Length of Time: 5–15 minutes

Materials: A gift for each child, wrapping paper, ribbons, etc.

Preparation: The gifts are wrapped, and a child's name is written on each. The gifts are then hidden.

Object of the Game: To find the gifts.

To Play:

Each child looks for the gift with his name on it. If he finds another's gift, he is to leave it alone and say nothing. When all the gifts have been found, the children open them.

Comment:

This is the best kind of treasure hunt, because everyone is guaranteed to find the treasure and no one is disappointed.

Nature Hunt

Number of Players: 6–30

Length of Time: 30–60 minutes

Materials: A paper bag for each team

Playing Site: Large park, woods, or field

Preparation: The leader prepares several lists of articles to be found at the playing site. There should be about the same number of articles on each list, but with little or no repetition from list to list. The articles might include: a red stone, a mosquito, a black-eyed Susan, a maple leaf, etc. They will vary depending on the area.

Object of the Game: To collect nature specimens.

To Play:

The leader divides the players into teams of 2 to 6 members each and gives each team a list of articles and a bag in which to collect them. The teams then branch out in search of their specimens. The players are not in a hurry, and are not competing with each other, so the teams may help each other, if necessary, to locate their assignments. When everything has been found, or a reasonable search has been made, the players do something artistic with their collection. For instance, they might make collages by team or as a whole group.

Jungle Breakfast

Number of Players: 3–12

Length of Time: 20–60 minutes

Materials: Breakfast food, dishes, etc.

Playing Site: The great outdoors

Preparation: The leader hides the breakfast food and paraphernalia in the grass, behind rocks, in trees, etc. This may include boxes of cereal, bowls, tablecloth, milk, etc., or even food that needs to be cooked, for a more ambitious activity.

Object of the Game: To find a meal in the wilderness.

To Play:

The leader tells the children that for breakfast they're going to live off the land. They are to search the wilds for food. As they are sent out for the search, the children will be delighted to find wilderness survival easier than expected. As they find the hidden treasure, they bring it back to camp until it is all found. The leader should take inventory to make sure all the provisions have been collected before the group settles down to enjoy their jungle breakfast.

Comment:

"Jungle Breakfast" is a natural camp game, but it is also effective as an early morning activity in a park or woods.

MIXERS AND FIRST-MEETING GAMES

Games to help people meet each other are provided here. "Getting to Know You," "Alliterative Attributes," "Name That Name," and "Picture Hunt" are helpful for learning names. "Churn and Chatter" and "Lucky Squares" will stimulate conversations. "Matchmaker Mixer," "Verse-Maker Mixer," "Scripture Mixer" and "Find That Tune" can be used to form pairs or small groups for another activity.

See Also:

Circle and Pass-It-On Games
Guessing Games
Reminiscing
Personal Photographs
Stunts

Getting To Know You

Number of Players: 10–30

Length of Time: 15–30 minutes

Object of the Game: To quote as many people as possible, citing their names correctly.

To Play:

The players sit in a circle. Someone makes a simple introductory statement, such as, "I am Randolph Lovelace, and I enjoy getting to know you." The player next to Randolph says, "I am Barbara Bright, and Randolph Lovelace says that he enjoys getting to know you." The player next to Barbara says, "I am George Grasshopper, and Barbara Bright says that Randolph Lovelace says that he enjoys getting to know you." The players continue the chain of quotations as long as possible. If the length gets unwieldy, they may start over with the next player, and, if they wish, a new statement.

Alliterative Attributes

Number of Players: 4–15

Length of Time: 10–60 minutes

Object of the Game: To think of a self-descriptive adjective.

To Play:

Each person tells the others his first name, followed by a self-descriptive adjective that begins with the first letter of his first name. An example is, "Ann, affectionate." The person briefly explains how the adjective applies to him.

Variations:

1. Participants choose two or three adjectives, using the first letters of their middle and/or last names as well as their first names.
2. Each person selects an adjective to describe the person next to him, rather than himself.

Comments:

Participants may need to be encouraged to use adjectives describing *positive* qualities. "Alliterative Attributes" helps participants get to know each other better and enhance their self-images.

Churn and Chatter

Number of Players: 10–100

Length of Time: 15–30 minutes

Material: Music-making apparatus

Preparation: The leader prepares a list of interesting conversation topics. The topics may be serious, such as "An event that changed my life," or absurd, such as "Why the sky should be green instead of blue."

Object of the Game: To converse with different people on a variety of subjects.

To Play:

The group divides in half and forms two circles, one within the other. When the music begins, the inner circle walks clockwise and the other circle walks counterclockwise. When the music stops, each player must converse with the player across from him in the other circle, on a topic announced by the leader. The music starts and stops several more times, obliging the players to walk, then stop and converse with new people on new topics as the leader directs.

Variation:

To aid players in getting to know more about each other, the leader announces that the person in each pair who lives farther away must start the conversation, or the person with more brothers and sisters, etc.

People-to-People

Number of Players: 8–30

Length of Time: 10–20 minutes

Object of the Game: To follow directions and find a new partner quickly.

To Play:

Each player finds a partner and joins the group in a circle, except for the leader who stands in the center. The leader snaps his fingers, chanting, "People to people," and the others join him. Whenever he desires, the leader changes his chant to "hand to hand", or "toes to toes", etc. The players must then touch their partners' hands with their hands, or toes with their toes, etc. The leader goes through various body parts, and then shouts, "People to people!" This is the signal for everyone to find a new partner, including the leader. One player is left without a partner, and becomes the new leader. Players try to have a different partner and a different leader each time.

Variation:

The game is more challenging (and probably more hysterical) if the leader names two different body parts, for example, "hand to foot."

Comments:

"People-to-People" is an excellent game for children of varying ages. Adults have fun changing partners frequently and having to find a new partner each time. If everyone works to arrange for a new leader each time, no one is considered the "odd man out" when it's his turn.

Lucky Squares

Number of Players: 10–100

Length of Time: 15–30 minutes

Materials: Large squares of cardboard, felt marker, paper and pen, bell or other noisemaker, prizes

Preparation: A different number is written on each cardboard square with felt marker. For each numbered square, a corresponding number is written on a small piece of paper. The cardboard squares are distributed around the floor.

Object of the Game: To be standing on a lucky square.

To Play:

The players walk around the room, pausing to shake hands and talk with other players while standing on the cardboard squares. At irregular intervals, the leader rings the bell or gives some other signal to draw everyone's attention. He then picks a number at random from his slips of paper. The piece of cardboard with that number on it is the "lucky square," and any player standing on that square wins a prize. The numbered paper is then returned to the other papers, so that the "lucky square" is always a surprise. "Lucky Squares" can be continued as long as time allows, or until all the prizes are distributed. For a Christian gathering, "blessed" may be substituted for "lucky."

Variation:

To encourage the participants to get to know new people, a bonus prize is given to players standing on a lucky square if they have just met each other.

Mixers

Name That Name

Number of Players: 10–30

Length of Time: 20–60 minutes

Materials: Paper, pencils and pins

Object of the Game: To figure out the names of the other
                          players.

To Play:

Each player is given a pencil, a pin, and several slips of paper.
On one slip of paper he writes his name, but omits every other
letter. Thus, Joseph Johnson might write his name, "J __
S __P __J __H __S __N __." He pins the name tag to himself.
The players mingle with each other, observing each other's
name tags. Each player tries to figure out the names of the
others, writing each guess on a slip of paper, and handing it
to the player named. The players do not look at the slips they
have been handed until the end of the game. When each player
has made a guess at each of the other's names, or sooner if
time demands, the players look at the names they have collected and read them aloud, announcing which one is cor-
rect.

Variation:

If many of the players know each other, names of famous
people may be substituted for the players' names.

Picture Hunt

Number of Players: 10–30

Length of Time: 20–60 minutes

Materials: Magazine pictures, cardboard, scissors, paste, tape, paper, and pencils

Preparation: Pictures of various objects are cut out of magazines and pasted on small pieces of cardboard. For each picture, a clue is listed, and a copy of the list is made for each player. The list might look like this:

Clue	Picture	Person's Name
1. The rat takes it		
2. A girl's best friend		
3. Etc.		

Object of the Game: To solve the riddles and learn people's names.

To Play:

A picture is taped to each player. Each player is also given a list of clues which he is to solve by mixing with the other players. When a player sees someone with a picture that fits one of the clues, he asks the person's name, then records the object pictured and the person's name in the square next to the clue. Thus, beside #1 he would write "cheese" and "John Smith." Beside #2 he would write "diamonds" and "Betty Brown." At an appropriate time, the leader asks someone with a completed list to read it, and makes corrections, if necessary.

Living Logo

Number of Players: 20–100

Length of Time: 20–40 minutes

Materials: Large cardboard squares, felt markers

Object of the Game: To form as many words with as many letters as possible.

To Play:

Each player writes the first letter of his last name on a piece of cardboard. The players then try to make words by lining up with their letters. Each time a group of players forms a word, they shout it and the others applaud. The players continue, trying to make their words as long as possible, until they have exhausted the possibilities or themselves.

Matchmaker Mixer

Number of Players: 10–100

Length of Time: 5–20 minutes

Materials: Pen and paper or index cards

Preparation: On each card one member of a famous duo is written, e.g., "Hansel" or "Romeo." The other members of the duos ("Gretel" and "Juliet") must appear on other cards.

Object of the Game: To find the other member of a famous duo.

To Play:

Each player is given a card with the name of a famous character. The cards may be affixed as name tags, if desired. The players then mingle until each has found the player with the character's name associated with his.

Variations:

1. Instead of famous duos, threesomes are used, such as Winkin', Blinkin', and Nod; or foursomes such as the Gospel writers.
2. A theme may be helpful, such as Bible characters, comedians, or presidential candidates.

Comment:

"Matchmaker Mixer" is a good way to prepare the group for another activity requiring partners or small groups.

Verse-Maker Mixer

Number of Players: 10–100

Length of Time: 30–90 minutes

Materials: Pens and paper

Preparation: Each of several pairs of rhyming words are written on separate pieces of paper.

Object of the Game: To find the rhyming word and create a short verse.

To Play:

Each player is given a word written on a piece of paper and is instructed to find the person whose word rhymes with his. Once they find each other, the rhyming partnership must create a poem using the two rhyming words—and additional rhyming words, if they wish. The players then read their poems to the whole group.

Variation:

Larger verse-making teams can be formed by distributing three or more words for each rhyme instead of only two.

Scripture Mixer

Number of Players: 10–100

Length of Time: 10–30 minutes

Materials: Well-known Scripture passages are selected, and verses from each one are written on separate slips of paper.

Object of the Game: To find people with Bible verses from the same passage.

To Play:

Each person is given a slip of paper with a small portion of a well-known Scripture passage, and is instructed to find other people with verses from the same passage. When such individuals find each other, they stick together until everyone has found his complement. Suggested passages are: 1 Corinthians 13, Psalm 23, the Ten Commandments, the Lord's Prayer—or choose more difficult ones as a challenge.

Comment:

If the verses are distributed carefully, people who don't know each other can be linked together.

Find That Tune

Number of Players: 8–30

Length of Time: 5–20 minutes

Object of the Game: To find the other players humming the same tune.

To Play:

The leader communicates, by a note or a whisper to each player, a tune he is to hum, so that there are a few players humming each of several tunes. The players then walk around humming until they find other players humming their respective tunes.

Comments:

"Find That Tune" makes a good party mixer and is also a good way to form small groups if that arrangement is needed for another activity.

CIRCLE AND PASS-IT-ON GAMES

Most of these games are quiet, sitting-down games that can be played almost anywhere. They can be used to supplement mixers at parties, and they also make ideal travel games.

See Also:

Anatomy
Getting to Know You
Alliterative Attributes
Churn and Chatter
The Scissors Game
The Broom Game
Storytelling Games

Word Chain

Number of Players: 2–30

Length of Time: 5–20 minutes

Object of the Game: To observe how one word leads to another.

To Play:

Players are seated in a circle. Someone begins by saying the first word that comes to his mind. The next player does the same, as does the next, and so on around the circle. It is interesting to see how the chain progresses, each word being suggested by the previous one. The chain may continue several times around the circle.

Rhyme Chain

Number of Players: 2–30

Length of Time: 5–30 minutes

Object of the Game: To rhyme a word as many times as possible.

To Play:

The first player says a word. The next player says a word that rhymes with the first person's word, and so does each successive player in turn. When someone can think of no more words that rhyme with the others, he says a new word and begins a new chain.

Comment:

"Rhyme Chain" is appropriate for a group of varying ages, and makes a good travel game.

Alphabetical Sentence

Number of Players: 1–26

Length of Time: 10–30 minutes

Object of the Game: To create an alphabetical sentence.

To Play:

The first player starts a sentence by saying a word beginning with "A." The next person adds the second word in the sentence, beginning the word with "B." The sentence continues, each player adding a word, until a long sentence has been created using the whole alphabet as the first letters of the words. If an impasse is reached, a player may begin a new sentence with the next alphabetical letter.

Variations:

1. The alphabet is reversed.
2. A random sentence is taken from a book, and the first letters of the words in the *created* sentence must correspond to the first letters of the words in the book.

First-Letter Linkup

Number of Players: 2–20

Length of Time: 10–30 minutes

Object of the Game: To build an alliterative story.

To Play:

The first player presents a short sentence in which all the major words begin with the same letter. Each successive player adds a word or words beginning with the same letter, each time repeating the whole sentence up to that point. More sentences and words are added, so that a story is created in which all the main words begin with the same letter. This will be quite a mouthful.

Comment:

Since all ages can enjoy "First-Letter Linkup," it makes a good family travel game.

I Packed My Trunk for China

Number of Players: 2–30

Length of Time: 10–30 minutes

Object of the Game: To recite everything being packed in the trunk and to think of a new item.

To Play:

The first player says, "I packed my trunk for China, and took an apple" (or "alligator" or any object that begins with "A"). The next player repeats the sentence, including the "A" word, and adds a "B" word. Each successive player recites the sentence with all the alphabetical items, adding one of his own. The players continue as long as they can, or until they have completed the alphabet.

Variations:

1. Items must belong to a certain category, such as fruit, musical instruments, vehicles, etc.
2. For additional challenge: two or three-word items are packed, beginning with A and B, then B and C, etc., such as "apple bread" and a "blue car." A three-word item might be a "big chocolate dog."

Comment:

"I Packed My Trunk for China" makes an excellent travel game.

Sentence Sounding

Number of Players: 4–20

Length of Time: 5–20 minutes

Object of the Game: To create entertaining sentences.

To Play:

One of the players makes a verbal sound of his choice, for example, "Fitzzz." Each of the other players uses the sound in a sentence, for example, "I put some fitzzz on my ice cream," or "Let's fitzzz again the way we did last summer." The other players then take turns creating new sounds for the group to use in sentences.

Telephone

Number of Players: 5–25

Length of Time: 10–30 minutes

Object of the Game: To see how a message changes when repeated many times.

To Play:

As players sit in a circle, someone whispers a message to the person next to him, who in turn repeats it to the next player, and so on around the circle. Each player whispers the message only once. When the message has completed its circuit, the last person repeats it aloud for comparison with the original message. The game is repeated so that as many players as possible can start messages.

Variations:

1. If a player can't understand the message at all, he may say "Operator?" to the player who whispered it. The whisperer then repeats the message once.
2. Players transmit the message *as quickly as possible* around the circle—no repeats allowed. This method is sure to produce a very different message at the end.
3. The leader whispers two messages, sending one to the right and one to the left. There is sure to be some confusion (and some laughter) when the messages cross on the other side.

Comment:

Little girls find "Telephone" delightful.

One Goes with the Other

Number of Players: 2–30

Length of Time: 5–30 minutes

Object of the Game: To make creative associations between objects.

To Play:

Players sit in a circle, and each privately brings an object of his choice to mind, such as "man," "mountain," "spoon," or anything. When everyone is ready, someone begins by disclosing the object he was imagining. The next person also discloses his object, then tells why his object goes with the first person's object. If the first object was "man" and the second one "mountain," the second person could say, "A man goes with a mountain because a man can move a mountain with faith." If the third person's object was "spoon," he might say, "A mountain goes with a spoon because some mountains have silver from which spoons are made." The associations may be as imaginative and farfetched as the players choose. The game may progress several times around the circle if desired.

District Attorney

Number of Players: 5–20

Length of Time: 15–30 minutes

Preparation: Leader of "District Attorney" creates an imaginary crime and prepares evidence of its commission.

Object of the Game: To develop an alibi and cast suspicion on another player.

To Play:

The District Attorney explains the crime to the other players and presents any evidence he has prepared. He then suggests why he suspects a certain player is guilty. The suspect player spontaneously develops an alibi. He explains why he happened to be there, why he may appear guilty, although he is not, and involves another player in his explanation so as to shift the blame. It is then the new suspect's turn to clear himself and pass on the blame. Play continues until all have been accused and have excused themselves.

Comments:

"District Attorney" is the most fun when players give creative, often complicated explanations. This creates humor and more of a challenge for the other players.

This Is a This

Number of Players: 6–30

Length of Time: 15–45 minutes

Materials: Two distinctly different objects

Object of the Game: To pass the objects completely around the circle in opposite directions.

To Play:

The players sit in a circle and recite the following dialogue as they pass the object around.

Leader: (He presents an object to player A on his left.) This is a this.

Player A: A what?

Leader: A this.

Player A: Oh. (He takes the object and presents it to the player B on his left.) This is a this.

Player B: A what?

Player A: (to leader) A what?

Leader: A this.

Player A: (to Player B) A this.

Player B: Oh. (He takes the object and presents it to player C on his left.) This is a this.

The chain of questions and answers continues until the object comes around to the leader again. Once the players have grown accustomed to the "This is a this" dialogue, they are ready for the introduction of the second object. The leader starts the "this" to his left and then immediately starts a "that" to the player on his right, announcing, "This is a that." Of course there will now be *two* chains of dialogue running back and forth, and the objects will have to cross at the other side of the circle! By that time, the players are usually laugh-

Mind Challengers

ing too hard to care, anyway. The game can continue with
other variations if the group can sustain the challenge.

Variations:

1. When "that" is passed, players must respond with "A
   which?" or "Huh?" instead of "A what?" They may also
   be required to say, "Thank you," instead of "Oh."
2. Instead of "this" and "that," the objects are identified as
   "thing" and "thang," or "which" and "what," or as tongue
   twisters such as "a pink and purple polka-dotted Ping-
   Pong paddle."
3. Two or more objects are introduced in each direction, with
   different names and responses required.
4. The question and response chain is recited *twice* before
   the object is passed. For example:

   Player A: This is a this.
   Player B: A what?
   Player A: A what?
   Leader: A this.
   Player A: A this.
   Player B: A what?
   Player A: A what?
   Leader: A this.
   Player A: A this.
   Player B: Oh.

5. Players are required to receive the objects with their left
   hands and to pass them with their right hands.

Comment:

Even young children can enjoy "This Is a This" if they are
part of a larger group of adults.

Funny Faces

Number of Players: 6–30

Length of Time: 10–20 minutes

Object of the Game: To repeat the funny face.

To Play:

The participants arrange themselves in a circle. An appointed player turns to the person next to him and makes a funny face or assumes a funny posture. That person then mimics the gesture (when he stops laughing), passing it on quickly to the next person, and so on around the circle. When funny face has completed the circuit, another person begins, until all have had a chance to initiate the face-making.

Add-an-Action

Number of Players: 4–30

Length of Time: 10–30 minutes

Object of the Game: To repeat all the actions in order.

To Play:

As the players stand in a circle, one of them makes a gesture of his choice, such as a wave, a jumping-jack, etc. Any bodily movement is acceptable. The player next to him must repeat his action and add one of his own. The next person repeats the first two actions in order and adds one of his *own*, and so on around the circle. Play continues until all players have added a motion or until the sequence is too long to be repeated correctly. The game can then begin anew.

Variation:

Sounds are made instead of motions.

Tactile Copier

Number of Players: 3–30

Length of Time: 5–30 minutes

Materials: Paper and pencil

Preparation: For each time the game is to be played, a simple diagram (such as a house, star, fish, etc.) is drawn on an index card or a small piece of paper.

Object of the Game: To copy the diagram correctly.

To Play:

The players arrange themselves in a line, all facing one way. A diagram is shown to the last person in line. This person uses his finger to reconstruct the image on the back of the person in front of him. Each player in turn passes the image on to the next person in line by tracing it on his back. The person at the head of the line draws the diagram on a piece of paper for the group to compare with the original drawing. The game can be repeated after the players rotate their positions.

Variations:

1. After passing on the image, each player draws the diagram as he perceives it. The group then compares their drawings.
2. Words can be traced instead of diagrams.

Comments:

Children especially enjoy this game of concentration. It's interesting to see how close (or how far) the final drawing is to the original.

Barrel of Monkeys

Number of Players: 7–25

Length of Time: 5–10 minutes

Materials: A prize (such as candy or a small gift)

Object of the Game: To capture the prize.

To Play:

The leader instructs the players, who are seated in a circle, that he will whisper the name of an animal to each of them. Each time he calls an animal name, the two players with that name are to run to the middle of the circle to try to grab the prize (before the other animal does) which the leader has placed there. The leader then whispers "monkey" in the ear of each player. He may then tease them by calling out "lions" or "tigers" (although of course no one will get up) before he says, "Monkeys!" and watches the whole group scramble chaotically. The sporting thing to do, of course, is to have a treat for all the monkeys to share afterward.

GUESSING GAMES

Guessing games are often played competitively, but can be easily modified by shifting the emphasis from individual to group success, or by refraining from scorekeeping. Many guessing games encourage creativity, such as "Finish the Mystery."

See Also:

Anatomy
Statues
Name That Name
Describo
Clever Cluing
Paraphrase
Songs Illustrated
Headlines
Telephone Directory Game
Bible Mime
One-Word Dramatics
Personal Photographs
People Collages
Tell Your Time
How Far?
Map Quiz

Object in Question

Number of Players: 4–20

Length of Time: 10–90 minutes

Object of the Game: To guess the object being discussed.

To Play:

Two players privately select an object in the room. They then discuss it with each other while the other players listen and try to guess what it is. When the object is discovered, another two players select an object.

Variation:

For an extra challenge, choose an object not in the room.

Teapot

Number of Players: 3–20

Length of Time: 15–60 minutes

Object of the Game: To discover the mystery verb.

To Play:

After one person leaves the room, the others choose a verb
that the person is to guess. When he returns, the person asks
questions of the other players, substituting the word "teapot"
for the verb; for example, "Do you teapot often?" He may make
guesses as to the actual verb as often as he likes between his
"teapot" questions. When he succeeds in guessing, another
person is chosen to leave the room.

Variations:

The players should decide before play begins which questioning style to use:
1. Yes-or-no questions and answers only.
2. Any kind of questions.
3. Responders may add comments to their yes-or-no answers.
4. Responders help the questioner if he is way off track, by
   being very specific or by reminding him of previous answers.

Comments:

Common verbs can be very difficult, especially if they have
more than one possible meaning. If the questions become
absurd, "teapot" can be quite hilarious.

Daffy Definitions

Number of Players: 4 or more

Length of Time: 15–30 minutes

Materials: Paper and pencils

Preparation: The leader consults a group of children in order to prepare the definitions. He reads each word of a list he has made up, and asks the children what the words mean. For each word, he writes a definition, word-for-word as the children say it, if possible.

Object of the Game: To guess the word corresponding to each definition.

To Play:

The leader brings his collection of child-made definitions to a group of adults, and distributes paper and pencils to all. As he reads each definition, everyone writes down the word he thinks is being defined. When all definitions have been read, the players share their guesses and the leader reveals the actual words corresponding to the definitions.

Finish the Mystery

Number of Players: 2–30

Length of Time: 15–60 minutes

Material: A book of short detective stories or mysteries.

Object of the Game: To figure out how the story ends.

To Play:

One person reads a story aloud, but stops just before the conclusion. The others try to figure out how the story ends, and offer their conjectures. The reader then finishes reading the story.

Variation:

Other kinds of stories besides mysteries are used. The object might be simply to create interesting endings rather than guess how the author finished the story.

One-Team Charades

Number of Players: 2–15

Length of Time: 10–90 minutes

Materials: Paper and pencils, three-minute timer

Object of the Game: To guess the subject being enacted.

To Play:

Each player writes, on separate slips of paper, one or two
subjects to be communicated. A subject may fall into one of
the following categories:

1. Books   4. Quotations
2. Movies   5. Songs
3. Famous People   6. Others of the group's choice

Each player initials his subjects and places them in a hat.
The players may then review standardized charades gestures,
or they may decide simply to improvise. Whatever method
they choose, only nonverbal methods of communication will
be allowed. The players take turns drawing a slip of paper at
random to communicate to the group. Before he begins, the
enactor reads the initials given, to signal the author not to
participate in the guessing. The group guesses as the enactor
makes various gestures, trying to identify the subject within
a three-minute period.

Variations:

1. The subjects are prepared beforehand by the party-plan-
   ners.
2. Each subject-author acts out his own subjects.

Machine Charades

Number of Players: 6–30

Length of Time: 20–60 minutes

Object of the Game: To guess the machine being acted out.

To Play:

The group is divided into teams of 3 to 6 players each. Each team confers privately to choose a machine they want to dramatize for the other teams. For example, the team might be a pinball machine, with one player as the ball bouncing off other team members, and another member operating the machine. When the teams have planned and perhaps rehearsed their machines, they reunite to present their machines and let the others guess what they are.

Variations:

1. Instead of dividing into teams, one person simply begins acting out part of a machine. When someone thinks he knows what the machine is, he acts as another part. The game continues until all are functioning parts of the machine. However, it may be discovered afterward that not everyone was thinking of the same machine!
2. Instead of dramatizing machines, situations or events are enacted, such as "white water rafting" or "a dog pound."

Comment:

"Machine Charades" is a marvelous game for including children with adults.

Clap-a-Rhythm

Number of Players: 2–30

Length of Time: 5–45 minutes

Object of the Game: To guess the song that is being clapped.

To Play:

The first player claps the rhythm of a song known to the other players, who then try to guess what it is. When the song is guessed, the next player takes his turn.

Variations:

1. A rhythm instrument is used instead of clapping.
2. The songs are limited to a category, such as Christmas carols or show tunes.

Comment:

"Clap-a-Rhythm" is a good filler while waiting for another activity.

Don't Look!

Number of Players: 3–20

Length of Time: 10–90 minutes

Object of the Game: To identify the change made.

To Play:

One player is selected to make a physical change in the room. He takes a moment to decide what he will do; for example, turn a book upside down. When he has decided, he says, "Don't look!" His command is the signal for the other players to close their eyes while he performs the change. When he has completed the action, he says, "You may look now." The other players try to guess what is different by studying the room and by asking yes-or-no questions. When they succeed, another person takes a turn at making a change.

Variation:

The person makes several changes, only one of which is the one to be identified. This "camouflage" version should be agreed upon at the beginning of the game.

Comments:

The person making the change should do it as quietly as possible. He may also wish to walk around the room while eyes are still closed to make his change harder to locate.

Quick-Change Artist

Number of Players: 2–200

Length of Time: 5–30 minutes

Object of the Game: To identify the changes made.

To Play:

The group is paired off. After the partners have had a chance to observe each other, each person turns his back to his partner and makes one or two changes in his appearance, e.g., untying a shoe, removing a barrette, etc. The partners then turn around and try to detect the changes in each other. The game can be repeated a few times before trying it with a new partner.

The Scissors Game

Number of Players:	4–20
Length of Time:	10–30 minutes
Materials:	A pair of scissors
Special Requirements:	Most of the players must be unfamiliar with the game.
Object of the Game:	To figure out the secret of passing the scissors "open" or "closed."

To Play:

The players seat themselves in a circle. The leader passes the scissors to the player beside him. If the leader's legs or ankles are crossed, he says, "I am passing the scissors closed." If his legs are not crossed, he says, "I am passing the scissors open." If the person to whom the leader passes the scissors knows the game, he can assist the demonstration by saying, "I am receiving the scissors open," if his legs are uncrossed; and if he crosses his legs before passing the scissors himself, he continues with, "and passing them closed." The scissors are passed around the circle. Each player announces how he believes he is receiving them, that is, "open" or "closed," and how he is passing them. The leader corrects them as necessary. The only requirement for passing or receiving the scissors "open" is to have uncrossed legs, and for passing or receiving them "closed" is to have crossed legs. At first, the leader and any others who know the game may say or do extraneous things (such as holding the scissors in different ways) to mislead the other players. But after the game has progressed, and most of the players have one by one quietly learned the pattern, they may find it necessary to cross and uncross their legs more conspicuously in order to help those

Secret Pattern Games

who are slower to understand. The game ends when everyone knows the secret.

Variation:

Instead of "open" and "closed," the scissors are passed "crossed" and "uncrossed."

The Broom Game

Number of Players: 3–20

Length of Time: 1–30 minutes

Material: A broom

Preparation: Most of the players must be new to the
                          game.

Object of the Game: To perform the broom trick correctly.

To Play:

The leader begins by clearing his throat and banging the broom on the floor, saying, "Gallagher grapes are very fine grapes, but I know some that are better." He then passes the broom to the person beside him, and asks the person to imitate his performance. After the person makes an attempt, the leader tells him whether it was "right" or "wrong." The broom is passed to the next player, and on around the group. Each time, the leader evaluates the performance as "right" or "wrong." The broom continues to be passed through the group until everyone is able to perform the trick correctly. The key to successfully performing the trick is the player clearing his throat before he recites the phrase. Any broombanging pattern is acceptable. As the trick is repeated correctly, more and more players will detect this, but it may be necessary to make the throat-clearing louder and more emphatic for players who are slower to notice.

Detective

Number of Players: 4–12

Length of Time: 20–30 minutes

Preparation: At least two players must be unfamiliar with the game.

Object of the Game: To solve a case supposedly created by the other players.

To Play:

Two people who have not played "Detective" before are appointed as the detectives. They are asked to leave the room while the group creates a case for them to solve. While the detectives are out, the leader tells the others that no case actually needs to be prepared. Instead, they are to listen carefully to the questions asked by the detectives. If the last word in the question ends with a vowel, "y" or "s," the group answers, "Yes." If the last word ends with a consonant other than "y" or "s," the group answers, "No." The detectives then return to the room and are allowed to ask yes-or-no questions of the group. Invariably they pursue an amazing story, which *they* are unwittingly creating. The story is completed by a detective asking a question such as, "Are we done?" Since "done" ends with a vowel, the group will reply, "Yes." The others then explain to the detectives how the story was created.

WORD GAMES

The challenge of these word games lies not only in playing them, but often in creating them. "Clever Cluing," "Paraphrase," and "Encrypted Messages" are particular examples.

See also:

Alliterative Attributes
Name That Name
Living Logo
Verse-Maker Mixer
Circle and Pass-it-on Games
Daffy Definitions
License-Plate Logo
License-Plate Lexicon

Group Scrabble®

Number of Players: 2–8

Length of Time: 45 minutes to 2 hours

Materials: Pencils, paper, Scrabble® game.

Object of Game: To maximize the group's score by placing appropriate words on the board in Scrabble® fashion.

To Play:

One player selects seven letter tiles and shows them to the group. Everyone in the group then tries to write down words that can be formed on the board using those letters. After about three minutes (or any other time interval agreed upon by the group) each person reads his list of words, and the highest scoring word is placed on the board. The letters used are replaced with new letters and the process begins again. Players can try to exceed the 500–700 point score which the Scrabble® rules say is "average."

Variations:

1. In addition to adding up the score of the words placed on the board, the group adds up the score of all words that are thought of. (If several players think of the same word, the word is only counted once.)
2. The group score is recorded, and the players try to surpass it the next time they play the game.

Comment:

Novice Scrabble® players have a chance to observe the techniques of more experienced players.

Describo

Number of Players: 2–10

Length of Time: 15–90 minutes

Materials: Pencils and index cards, timer or watch with a second hand

Preparation: Each index card becomes a "category card." Eight words belonging to the same category are listed on each card. For example, a color category card might list red, blue, green, etc. Other categories might be: parts of the body, famous cities, holidays, etc. These cards can be prepared by the leader beforehand or by the players themselves just before playing. At least 8 to 10 cards should be prepared.

Object of the Game: To guess all the words of a category within a minute.

To Play:

A player selected as the first clue-giver takes a category card and tries to describe each word listed, using gestures and one-word clues. For example, clues for "red" might be blood, fire, brick, etc. The other members of the group call out their guesses until someone says the listed word. The clue-giver continues through the list until one minute has passed. Each player takes a turn as the clue-giver, and the group repeatedly tries to meet the one-minute deadline to guess all eight words in the category.

Variation:

No time limit is set; the goal is simply to guess all the words in the category.

Comments:

"Describo" can be played by all ages. It is important to make words challenging, but within the language abilities of those playing.

Clever Cluing

Number of Players: 2–50

Length of Time: 30–60 minutes

Materials: Paper and pencils

Object of the Game: To determine the hidden meanings of phrases.

To Play:

One person suggests a category (e.g., professional football teams, major streets, well-known American cities, nations of the world, houschold appliances, etc. Individually or in small groups, players devise word-plays or other clues which uniquely pertain to the names of items fitting the suggested category. (See example below.) The leader then offers one or two clues at a time, and the whole group tries to determine which item the clue reveals.

Example:

Each of the following clues is a description or restatement of the nickname of a National Football League team, such as the "Lions," the "Chargers," the "Falcons," etc.

1. Six Monarchs
2. Numbers You Can Remember
3. Servants of God
4. Indian Leaders
5. Seven Squared
6. Sun-Tanned Bodies
7. Deficit Spender
8. Endures
9. Queues
10. Lubricators
11. Marauding Attackers
12. High-Ranking Boy Scouts
13. American Gauchos
14. They Fill Suitcases, Don't They?

15. Army Insects
16. Were Girls
17. Male Sheep
18. Flippers for Plastic People
19. Corn for a Dollar

20. Point-After Melees
21. Faster Than a Speeding Bullet

22. Hot Epidermis
23. Six-Shooters
24. Thieves
25. Tell, Shakespeare and the Conqueror
26. Oceangoing Predators
27. Rodeo Animals
28. Autumn Prisoners

Variations:

1. The clues are devised ahead of time. They can be put before the group one or two at a time, as above; or if the game is to be played silently or on an individual basis, each participant can be given the entire list of clues.
2. Participants just offer their clues as they think of them.

Comment:

"Clever Cluing" provides an opportunity for punsters to ply their trade in a socially acceptable manner.

Salt and Pepper

Number of Players: 3–10

Length of Time: 15–30 minutes

Materials: Pencils and paper

Object of the Game: To create nonduplicative lists of paired words.

To Play:

During a fixed period of time—perhaps three minutes—each player creates a list of words that are customarily used together, e.g., salt and pepper, cars and trucks, etc. In doing so, he tries to record pairs that no one else is likely to list. When the time is up, each player reads his list of pairs, and finds out if any other player has recorded the same words. The group can repeat the game, each time trying to compile the largest accumulation of pairs with the least duplication. It may help to limit the subject matter for each round—for instance, round one: foods; round two: historical figures; round three: natural phenomena.

Paraphrase

Number of Players: 2–12

Length of Time: 5–20 minutes

Object of the Game: To create word-plays with the prefix "para."

To Play:

When a player thinks of a riddle definition, he speaks it out for the others to solve. Each riddle will be "two . . ." The solution will be "para-_____." Examples are:

Riddles	Solutions
Two physicians	Paradox
Two mouthwashes	Periscope
Two Scandinavians	Paraffin

The players voice the solutions as they think of them, or take turns. The game can continue as long as imaginations permit.

Variation:

Other prefixes are used, such as "dia." For this a riddle might be, "To color a tree," the solution being "dialogue."

Encrypted Messages

Number of Players: 2 and up

Length of Time: 30–90 minutes

Materials: Pencils, paper, masking tape, and
                          pieces of smooth cardboard or other
                          material that can be written on, taped
                          over, and untaped with minimal tear-
                          ing.

Object of the Game: To decipher an encoded message.

To Play:

Each person is given the name of a different member of the
group, who will be the recipient of his "encrypted message."
He then composes a brief (10–30 word) upbuilding message
which he will be writing in code for that person. To prepare
the message, each player:

1. Writes the recipient's name on the piece of cardboard (to
   avoid confusing the codes later).
2. Writes the alphabet in order on the cardboard, all in one
   line.
3. Writes all the letters again, in random order, putting each
   letter underneath one of the original letters.
4. Writes the message on paper, substituting the random
   letters for the alphabetical ones. The message is now written in code.
5. Covers the cardboard letters with masking tape.

The messages are then given to the recipients, who decipher
them by trial and error, logic, intuition, and (if they so desire)
by uncovering some or all the letters on the cardboard. The
following tips may be given:

1. The shortest words are easiest to start with. For instance, one-letter words are usually "I" or "a." Two-letter words are usually a consonant and a vowel.
2. The letters that appear the most are usually A, E, I, O, S, T, N, R and L.
3. Consonants and vowel patterns can be detected, such as words ending with vowel-consonant-silent "e," or plurals ending with "s" or "es."
4. When three or four letters of long words are known, the whole word can be guessed.
5. Sentence structure indicates whether a word is likely to be a noun, verb, adjective, etc.
6. It's helpful to make lots of guesses, being prepared to change them later.

Variations:

1. Players decipher in pairs instead of individually.
2. Instead of writing an encoded message, the letters of each word are jumbled. For example, "This is a jumble" could be written, "hist si a bejlmu." The jumble can be made more difficult by rearranging the words within the sentence as well.

Comments:

"Encrypted Messages" is a good activity for school-aged children (or adults) on a long car trip. It is a fairly quiet game, requiring little personal interaction.

CREATIVE GAMES

"Describe and Draw" challenges concentration and listening skills. "Songs Illustrated," "Headlines," and "Telephone Directory Game" require imagination and some guessing. "Scripture Memory Game" is a clever, fun way to learn some Bible passages. "Greasy Spoon" is imaginative and just a trifle silly, but hopefully delicious as well.

See Also:

> *Picture Letters*
> *Word Games*
> *Dramatic Games*
> *Rhythm and Music Games*
> *Storytelling Games*
> *People Collages*

Songs Illustrated

Number of Players: 2–15

Length of Time: 15–60 minutes

Materials: Paper and colored pencils, pens, markers or crayons

Object of the Game: To create a picture suggested by a song.

To Play:

Each player makes a picture illustrating a song of his choice; then shows it to the others, who try to identify the song represented.

Variations:

1. The pictures are collected and exhibited one at a time by the leader. The players try to guess not only the song, but who drew the picture.
2. Book titles or Bible passages are illustrated.
3. Scripture references are written on slips of paper. Each player draws one from a hat, looks it up, and illustrates it.

Describe and Draw

Number of Players: 3–50

Length of Time: 15–45 minutes

Materials: One or more prepared designs, paper and pencil for everyone

Preparation: One or more designs are prepared, consisting of several lines and shapes. It is better to start with simple designs, then move on to more complicated figures.

Object of the Game: To reproduce a design by following oral instructions.

To Play:

One player is given a design (example below) which he then describes to the other players, using oral instructions only. No drawing or gesturing, etc., by the instructor is allowed. The others individually attempt to reproduce the design, then compare their results with the original drawing. Others may take turns being the instructor.

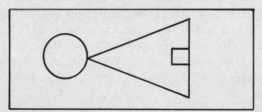

Comment:

It's interesting to see how differently a series of instructions can be interpreted.

Headlines

Number of Players: 4–15

Length of Time: 20–60

Materials: Pencils and paper

Preparation: A list of nursery rhymes or stories is prepared.

Object of the Game: To imagine headlines for well-known stories.

To Play:

The leader reads his list of well-known nursery rhymes or stories, pausing between titles while each player writes down an imaginary newspaper headline for each one. For instance, "Three Blind Mice" might inspire the headline: "Handicapped Rodents Injured by Rural Woman." The players then take turns reading the headlines they have written. The game can be repeated using fairy tales, Bible stories, historical events, etc.

Variations:

1. Instead of reading their own headlines, the players exchange lists, or write the headlines on small slips of paper to be collected and drawn from a hat and read by the leader.
2. Instead of the leader preparing a list, each player thinks of a headline for the nursery rhyme of his choice. The other players try to guess the rhyme that goes with each headline.

Comment:

The headlines can be saved and presented to another group, who try to guess what the headlines are describing.

Telephone Directory Game

Number of Players: 4–12

Length of Time: 20–90 minutes

Materials: Telephone directory, paper and pencil

Preparation: The leader finds a name from each of several categories from the directory, such as a man's name, a woman's name, a restaurant, a dancing school, etc. He tries to find names that are particularly interesting or unusual.

Object of the Game: To create imaginary directory entries; and to guess names that are listed in the directory.

To Play:

As the leader announces the categories, the players write down imaginary names for each one, without disclosing them to each other. Each player hands their imaginary-names list to the leader. The leader then reads the imaginary names for a given category, randomly inserting the real name. The others try to identify the real name from the directory. The leader then tells the group which was the actual name.

Variation:

Instead of being selected ahead of time by the leader, the players each take turns finding an unusual name.

Comment:

Depending on the size of the community, it may be necessary to use another city's directory to avoid familiarity with names and businesses.

Scripture Memory Game

Number of Players: 4–20

Length of Time: 30–90 minutes

Materials: Several Bibles in different translations, pens and paper

Object of the Game: To memorize Scripture by creative
means.

To Play:

The players are divided up into teams of 2 to 4 members each.
Each team selects a Bible verse and creates a way to help the
larger group memorize it. The players may wish to put the
verse to music, act it out, make a picture of it, or use any
other means they can imagine. Various translations may be
consulted to find the one that best suits their method. The
team members should memorize the verse themselves, to
make sure their method works. Each team then presents its
verse to the others, and the whole group learns the verse.
When all the teams have made their presentations, the whole
group repeats the verses learned, to make sure they still remember them.

Comment:

People who think they are not good at memorizing Scripture
may find a means to do so.

Greasy Spoon

Number of Players: 3–20

Length of Time: 1–2 hours

Materials: Food, utensils, etc., as described on the menu; a menu for each guest

Preparation: Two or more people may wish to prepare the menu and selections, which is almost as much fun as serving the meal.

Object of the Game: To enjoy a surprise meal ordered from a mixed-up menu.

To Prepare Menu:

Each dish to be offered, as well as utensils, napkins, etc., are disguised on the menu with fancy names. The planners decide what they will serve, and think of a phony name for each item. For example, a menu might read:

1. Cleopatra's Needle	5. Bloodshot Eyes
2. Running Rabbit	6. Old Faithful
3. Haymaker	7. White Lightning
4. Laplander's Delight	8. Dirty Deal

And be translated in the kitchen to:

1. Toothpick	5. Green Olives
2. Carrot	6. Water
3. Fork	7. Milk
4. Napkin	8. Coffee

There should be 20 to 30 items on the menu. The diners are given request forms along with their menus and are asked to request four items for each of three courses. They are not

told, however, that some items are actually eating utensils.
The request forms might look like this:

First Course	Second Course	Third Course
1.	1.	1.
2.	2.	2.
3.	3.	3.
4.	4.	4.

After all the orders are taken, the guests are served the meal,
one course at a time. They will gasp and laugh at what they
are served, and sometimes look with envy at what others are
served. Some dishes might look delicious, but difficult to eat,
because the proper utensils were not ordered. When the crazy
meal is finished, the guests might be offered their choice of
undisguised selections.

DRAMATIC GAMES

From the very simple "One-Word Dramatics" to the full-scale "Your Own Radio Broadcast," these games are enjoyable for all ages in any situation.

See Also:

Caterpillar Over the Mountain
My Ship Has Come In
Story Stretch
District Attorney
Machine Charades
Scripture Memory Game
Label Me

Paper-Bag Skits

Number of Players: 6–30

Length of Time: 30–90 minutes

Materials: Large paper bags and assorted objects

Preparation: A bag for each team is filled with several unrelated objects. These can be almost anything, e.g., a wooden spoon, a screw, a bar of soap, and a telescope. It's nice to have one object for each team member.

Object of the Game: To present a skit using all the props provided.

To Play:

Each three- to six-member team is given a bag and is told to prepare a skit using all the objects in the bag as props. The props may be used as they would be in normal life, or they may be imaginatively employed. For instance, a vase might become a vial of poison. When all the skits have been planned and rehearsed, they are performed for the amusement of all.

Variations:

1. Stipulations are given regarding the type of skits performed, e.g., humorous, serious, acting out a parable, a moral, or a proverb.
2. The bags are filled with costumes instead of props (e.g., a pair of Groucho Marx glasses, a wig, a long dress, and a pair of gloves). Each actor must perform in costume.
3. Five bags are prepared, one labeled "who," another labeled "what," another "when," another "where," another "why."

In each bag are placed pieces of paper with information appropriate to the bag's category; e.g., "where" would have a different location written on each piece of paper. Each individual or group draws a paper from each of the five bags. They then act out a short scene or story using the five given components, with or without rehearsal. Lots of encouragement should be given the actors.

Bible Mime

Number of Players: 6–30

Length of Time: 20–90 minutes

Object of the Game: To guess the Bible story portrayed in the pantomime.

To Play:

Teams of three to six members each select one or more biblical events to pantomime for the other players. Sound effects are allowed, but no speaking. The others try to identify the Bible stories being enacted.

Variations:

1. Scripture passages are cited on slips of paper and drawn from a hat for performance.
2. Modern-day versions of Bible stories are dramatized. In this case, the actors are allowed to speak, and guessing will probably not be necessary to identify the stories.
3. Modern-day or pantomime versions of nursery rhymes or fairy tales are enacted.

One-Word Dramatics

Number of Players: 3–20

Length of Time: 10–45 minutes

Preparation: A variety of emotions are written on slips of paper. Examples: hate, mirth, heartbreak, envy, joy, anger.

Object of the Game: To present dramatic expressions.

To Play:

One by one, each player draws a slip of paper and dramatically enacts the word written on it in whatever manner he sees fit.

Variations:

1. Fruit of the Spirit are used instead of emotions.
2. The audience tries to guess the word being portrayed.

Your Own Radio Broadcast

Number of Players: 6–20

Length of Time: 60–90 minutes

Materials: A tape recorder, blank tape, and a separate room for each group

Object of the Game: To prepare an imaginary radio broadcast.

To Play:

Each group of 3 to 5 people is asked to record an imaginary radio broadcast. The performances are completely subject to the players' creativity. They may include newscasts, music, comedy, drama, political speeches, commercials, or whatever. Sound effects might enhance the recordings, such as a ringing telephone or a creaking door. At an agreed-upon time the groups reconvene to hear each others' recordings.

Variations:

1. Each group is given a bag of noisemaking objects which they must use for sound effects as part of the broadcast.
2. Instead of recording the broadcasts, the performances are live. A blanket or screen is set up, behind which the players "broadcast."

RHYTHM AND MUSIC GAMES

These games should not be limited to players with musical experience. In fact, many offer an ideal setting for developing consciousness of rhythm and music. "Clap and Miss," "Human Frogs," and "Glass Band" are examples.

See Also:

Listening Test
Nonelimination Musical Chairs
I Made a Tasty Cake
Churn and Chatter
People-to-People
Find That Tune
Clap-a-Rhythm
Songs Illustrated
Scripture Memory Game
Your Own Radio Broadcast
Motorcar Medley

Clap and Miss

Number of Players: 2–200

Length of Time: 10–30 minutes

Preparation: The leader must have a good sense of
                          rhythm.

Object of the Game: To repeat a clapping rhythm correctly.

To Play:

The leader performs a series of hand claps and "misses" for
the group to repeat. A "miss" means that the hands begin
the clapping motion, but instead of meeting each other to
clap, one hand passes over the top of the other in midair so
that they "miss." Each clap or miss is equivalent to one beat.
Virtually any rhythm can be composed by claps and misses
(similar to musical notes and rests). The leader should be
sensitive to the abilities of the group and increase the com-
plexity of the rhythms for more challenge. He may either ver-
balize the pattern by saying, for instance, "clap, clap, miss,
clap," and then perform it with them; or merely demonstrate
it for them to repeat. The group works to improve its skill,
but is often amused when mistakes occur anyway.

Continuous Rhythm

Number of Players: Groups of 8

Length of Time: 15–45 minutes

Object of the Game: To keep a clapping rhythm going.

To Play:

Each group of eight players pairs off, then numbers its pairs one through four. Each pair practices the following hand-clap rhythm, one beat per clap: clap over head, clap behind back, clap in front, clap hands with partner. The group then begins its continuous rhythm. Pair #1 begins the rhythm as practiced. When pair #1 is on the second beat (behind back), pair #2 begins the rhythm. When pair #2 is on the second beat, pair #3 begins, then pair #4. If the group is functioning correctly, each pair will always be performing a different motion. The group continues, speeding up until the rhythm breaks down, or until they wish to try the more complex rhythm of the variation below.

Variation:

This rhythm can be done with eight pairs instead of four. It may remind the players of "Pease Porridge Hot."
1. Clap thighs
2. Clap in front
3. Clap right hand with partner's right
4. Clap in front
5. Clap left hand with partner's left
6. Clap in front
7. Clap both hands with partner's
8. Clap in front

Comments:

Some groups will enjoy "Continuous Rhythm" for the challenge of maintaining the rhythm and other groups for the amusement provided when the rhythm breaks down.

Chock Chiddle Po Po

Number of Players: Groups of 4

Length of Time: 10–30 minutes

Object of the Game: To maintain motions while chanting in rhythm.

To Play:

Within each group of four the players are numbered 1,2,3, and 4. Everyone chants together, "Chock chiddle, chock chiddle, chock chiddle po po," several times in rhythm. At the beginning of one of the repetitions, the leader begins a motion, such as patting his head, skipping in place, or grimacing. All #1 players must imitate him. At the beginning of the next verse, he starts a new motion for #2 players to follow. Number 1 players continue their assigned motion. With each repetition of the verse, the leader starts a new motion for the next numbered players until all are contributing. Once players are used to the rhythm, the game is made more challenging by changing motions with each verse. Verse #1: Player #1 does motion #1. Verse #2: Player #1 does motion #2, player #2 does motion #1. Verse #3: Player #1 does motion #3, player #2 does motion #2, player #3 does motion #1, etc.

Comments:

"Chock Chiddle Po Po" will be increasingly amusing if the leader keeps changing the motions, particularly if he instructs the players to keep absolutely serious faces.

Human Frogs

Number of Players: 6–200

Length of Time: 10–20 minutes

Object of the Game: To enjoy a choral effect.

To Play:

The group is divided into three sections, each of which is given a part to rehearse. Section A sings in a high, staccato voice, "Tomatoes, tomatoes, tomatoes. . ." Section B sings, a little more slowly in a medium pitch, "Potatoes, potatoes, potatoes. . ." Section C sings in a very slow, low, legato, "Fried bacon, fried bacon, fried bacon. . ." When all have rehearsed, the sections sing their parts simultaneously for an extraordinary choral performance. The sections may then rotate parts if they wish.

Variation:

Other lyrics may be substituted according to the director's or the singers' imagination.

Musical Poses

Number of Players: 3–100

Length of Time: 10–30 minutes

Material: Live or recorded music

Object of the Game: To be suspended in amusing poses.

To Play:

The leader instructs the others to move in ways appropriate to the music he is playing—a march, modern dance, musical game such as "London Bridges," or whatever. Exaggerated movements and creativity are encouraged. When the leader stops the music, the players must freeze in whatever position they are in. Everyone then looks around to observe the often comical poses in which the others have been captured. The music resumes until the leader finds another opportune point to interrupt the movements. He may continue to interrupt and change the style of music as he sees fit.

Song Chain

Number of Players: 2–12

Length of Time: 10–60 minutes

Object of the Game: To keep singing as long as possible without breaking the chain.

To Play:

A player begins singing a song while others listen carefully to the words. When another player hears a word sung that he knows to be in a different song, he breaks in, singing the new song. The original singer stops while the new singer continues, and again all watch for an opportunity to start a new song. If a song is completed before anyone breaks in, someone just thinks of another song and starts over.

Variations:

1. Players take turns offering new songs instead of volunteering them randomly.
2. If children are playing, they might enjoy the song chain more if each child has a chance to finish his song, rather than being interrupted.

Comments:

"Song Chain" is an excellent way to pass the time riding in a car, or waiting for the next activity.

The Lyrics Are Yours

Number of Players: 4–30

Length of Time: 30–60 minutes

Materials: Pencils and paper, musical instrument (optional)

Preparation: Someone with some musical ability composes a song without words to be presented to the group. An alternative to this is to find an old song that none of the players is apt to know.

Object of the Game: To write lyrics to the music presented.

To Play:

The leader or designated musician plays or hums the music prepared. It is up to each person or team to write words to fit the music. When everyone is ready, the various lyrics are sung by their authors for the enjoyment of the whole group. If the music was taken from an actual song, the original lyrics can then be sung.

Variation:

The various lyrics are all sung by the leader. The others then try to guess which person or team wrote which words.

Group Songwriters

Number of Players: 2–20

Length of Time: 15–45 minutes

Materials: Pencil and paper (optional)

Object of the Game: To write a song as a group.

To Play:

The first player simply makes up the first line for a song and sings it. The second person follows with another line, the next person with another, and so on, until three, four, or even eight lines have been sung, enough to be considered a spontaneously created song. The whole group then sings the song together. The game should be repeated at least enough to give everyone a turn. As the budding composers get practiced, they may wish to develop their style according to the variations below.

Variations:

1. The first few lines are considered the chorus, to be repeated after each new verse created.
2. Certain rhyme and rhythm patterns must be followed.
3. A theme is chosen, such as a holiday, or a picture is used to inspire the lyrics.
4. Instead of a whole line, only a word or two is sung at a time.
5. The music is composed first, and the words are supplied by other players. The lyricists might even write their words in seclusion from the composers. They then must try to match their words to the music!

Glass Band

Number of Players: 4–12

Length of Time: 20–90 minutes

Materials: Glass tumblers, pencils, water, sheet music to familiar songs

Preparation: The glasses are filled to varying degrees with water, so that each glass will sound a different note when struck. This should be done by carefully matching their pitches with a piano or other instrument.

Object of the Game: To make music with water glasses.

To Play:

Each participant is given a pencil, music, and responsibility for one or more glasses. The leader tells the musicians which note is sounded by each glass and shows them how to read the music. The musicians will probably want to circle the note they are to play. The leader then rehearses the group through each of the songs, each musician striking his glass or glasses at the proper time.

Comments:

"Glass Band" is an excellent way to introduce music reading and performance to the inexperienced. It can be used as a variety act for a Christmas program or other special occasion.

STORYTELLING GAMES

Most of these are variations of "Continuous Story," a vehicle for a group-created story.

See Also:

> *What Comes Next?*
> *Story Stretch*
> *Finish the Mystery*
> *Personal Photographs*

Trouble-Shooters

Number of Players: 4–40

Length of Time: 10–60 minutes

Materials: Paper and pencils

Object of the Game: To create unusual solutions to imaginary problems.

To Play:

The group is divided in half and is seated in two lines. The players in one line each write a description of an imaginary problem. The other players each write an imaginary solution, without comparing notes with the problem writers. A sample problem might be: "I bailed out of an airplane and found myself falling over a snake pit." A sample solution might be: "So, I left the country and settled in a small Italian town." When everyone is ready, the first problem-writer reads his description. The first player in the solution-writing line then reads his solution to the problem. It will probably sound completely absurd! Each player in turn reads his problem or solution, often resulting in hysterical laughter. When all the problems and solutions have been read, the writers may reverse roles for the next game.

Variations:

1. Players might find it easier to write solutions when they have a problem in mind. Each player writes a problem, then, on a separate piece of paper, its solution. Each player, in turn, reads only the problem, and lets the next player read his solution.
2. Instead of forming lines, the descriptions are passed to the leader, who alternately reads problems and solutions at random.

Continuous Story

Number of Players: 3–15

Length of Time: 15–60 minutes

Object of the Game: To create a story to which all have contributed.

To Play:

The first person begins to tell a story, but after a few sentences he stops (perhaps even in mid-sentence) to let the person on his left continue it. The person on his left develops the story a little more, and then stops to give the next person a turn. The players all contribute to the plot in this fashion until everyone has had one or several turns. The story is concluded by the last player with a happy ending, a lesson, or other suitable resolution.

Variations:

1. Providing a picture as a basis for the story makes "Continuous Story" especially fun for children.
2. Each player ends his turn with a predicament for the next person to resolve.
3. Players are directed to tell a particular type of story, e.g., humorous, inspiring, mystery or science fiction. If the story is to be humorous, players should be cautioned against extreme silliness unless that is acceptable to the group.
4. Similar games are "Ghost Writers," "Novel Objects," and "Ten Talents."

Ghost Writers

Number of Players: 4–10

Length of Time: 40–90 minutes

Materials: A picture from a magazine, paper and pencils, and a three-minute timer

Object of the Game: To create humorous stories.

To Play:

A picture is placed in view of all the players, so that they can each begin to form a story idea based on it. After a minute or two, the timer is set for three minutes. Each player proceeds to write his story based on the picture. When the three-minute period is up, all players must stop writing, be it mid-sentence or even mid-word, and pass their papers to the left. When players have silently read the new stories passed to them, the timer is set again for three minutes. Each player now continues the story in front of him until the next signal to pass it on. The game continues until the players have their original stories passed back to them. Players then read the stories aloud which are usually hysterically funny.

Novel Objects

Number of Players: 4–12

Length of Time: 20–60 minutes

Materials: An object for each player and a paper bag for each object

Preparation: Several unrelated objects are collected and concealed in separate paper bags.

Object of the Game: To create a story incorporating various props.

To Play:

Each player is given a paper bag containing an object to include in his portion of the tale. He does not reveal his object, however, until it is his turn to speak. The first person begins to tell a story involving his object, but after a few sentences he stops (perhaps even mid-sentence) to let the person on his left continue it. The result is usually a very funny story.

Ten Talents

Number of Players: 4–10

Length of Time: 30–90 minutes

Object of the Game: To create an adventure story featuring the storytellers.

To Play:

Each member of the group is asked to give a positive one-word description of the person on his right. Only when all have shared their descriptions are they told that they will be creating a story in which they are the characters. One of the players begins by describing a mission on which the characters are to be sent as a task-solving team. Each of the players takes a turn at developing the story, keeping the characters (themselves) consistent with the one-word descriptions mentioned earlier. These qualities, it turns out, are just the ones needed to execute the mission! The story is complete when the mission is accomplished and everyone has had a chance to contribute to the telling.

Comment:

"Ten Talents" encourages its participants by demonstrating the value of their personal gifts.

RELATIONSHIP-BUILDING GAMES

These games are invaluable. They combine fun with deepening understanding and building self-esteem. Every group that wants to grow should include some of these from time to time.

See Also:

Encrypted Messages
Ten Talents

Reminiscing

Number of Players: 3–15

Length of Time: 10–90 minutes

Materials: Paper and pencils

Preparation: On each slip of paper, a story cue is written, such as, "Your first time away from home," or "Your scariest childhood experience." This can also be done by the players themselves just before they begin the game. There should be one to three cues per player.

Object of the Game: For the participants to get to know each other better.

To Play:

The first storyteller draws a slip of paper, takes a minute or two to think, then tells a story from his past, prompted by the cue he has drawn. The story should last 3 to 5 minutes, but exceptions can be made. Each of the others does the same, as many times as desired.

Variation:

Instead of experiences, family traditions or customs are explained, such as holiday activities, vacations, visiting relatives, doing household chores or playing games.

Comments:

The game is made most effective by attentive listeners and follow-up questioning, when appropriate. Sometimes a good story will inspire a similar one by one of the listeners. "Reminiscing" is any easy get-to-know-each-other game, because everyone is an expert on his own past, and most people love to talk about themselves.

Personal Photographs

Number of Players: 3–15

Length of Time: 15–90 minutes

Materials: A photograph of each player

Preparation: Each participant is asked to bring a photograph of himself; childhood pictures are usually the best.

Object of the Game: For the players to get to know each other better, and enjoy interesting stories.

To Play:

One by one, each player shows his photograph to the others, and shares an interesting experience connected with it; or just tells something about his life when he was the age pictured. The others listen attentively and may ask questions when he is finished.

Variations:

1. Before the sharings are given, the players try to guess which childhood picture belongs to whom.
2. The photos are exchanged, and each person makes up a story about the picture he is given. The pictures are then returned to the original owners and the true stories are told.

Interdependence

Number of Players: 3–12

Length of Time: 15–30 minutes

Materials: String, scissors, pitcher of water and cups for everyone

Playing Site: Outdoors or a spacious room that will not be damaged by water.

Object of the Game: To perform a task cooperatively.

To Play:

Every player has his left hand tied to the right hand of the player on his left, and his right hand tied to the left hand of the player on his right. The tied-up group then distributes a drink of water to each of its members, and performs any other tasks that its members wish to attempt.

Comments:

"Interdependence" reminds the group that we are members one of another in the Body of Christ.

Yarn Circle

Number of Players: 3–12

Length of Time: 5–20 minutes

Material: Ball of yarn

Object of the Game: To create a symbolic pattern out of yarn.

To Play:

The players stand in a circle. As one player holds the ball of yarn, he tells the others something he is thankful for. He then throws the ball of yarn to another player, but keeps holding on to the end. The other players do likewise after catching the ball of yarn, each retaining a bit of the yarn, and holding it taut, so that a beautiful pattern is created. When everyone has tossed the yarn at least once, a few members drop their yarn. The remaining yarn-holders must then back up to pick up the slack. The "Yarn Circle" can be repeated once or twice before its symbolism is explained: When everyone contributes to the group, a beautiful pattern is created. But as people drop out, the pattern suffers, and those that remain end up farther apart.

Label Me

Number of Players: 5–50

Length of Time: 10–30 minutes

Materials: Pen, paper, yarn, scissors, tape

Preparation: Strips of paper are cut, and various personality traits are written on them, such as "angry," "shy," "generous," etc. The strips are taped to pieces of yarn which will be wrapped around people's heads.

Object of the Game: To learn how different personalities are treated.

To Play:

A label is tied to each person's forehead so that others can read it, but the bearer cannot. The players then interact, relating to each other as they would to people with the traits on the labels. At a designated time, the players remove their labels and discuss their experience. The following questions may be helpful: Could they figure out their traits by the way others related to them? How did it make them feel about themselves and others? Are there ways they should change the ways they relate to people?

Variations:

Instead of personality traits, other categories are used:
1. Relatives: Grandma, kid sister, rich uncle, etc.
2. Occupations: Minister, movie star, doctor.
3. Religions: Jew, fundamentalist, atheist, etc.

Forgiveness Exercise

Number of Players: 2–20

Length of Time: 15–45 minutes

Preparation: Ten sample situations of wrongs committed are listed on a chalkboard, or copies are made for distribution. The situations should vary in gravity.

Examples might be:
1. A ten-year-old steals money from his mother's purse.
2. An unemployed father steals shoes for his children to wear to school.
3. A teenage boy breaks into an invalid women's home and steals her jewelry.
4. A secretary steals time from her job by taking an extra long lunch hour.

Object of the Game: To grow in being able to forgive.

To Play:

Participants are asked to consider the list of wrongs, and to individually decide which three they find easiest to forgive and which three they find hardest. After they have made their choices, the group breaks down into clusters of 2 to 5 persons each to share why they answered as they did and to consider how God looks at the situations.

People Collages

Number of Players: 4–12

Length of Time: 30–90 minutes

Materials: Old magazines, scissors, paste, construction paper

Object of the Game: To create a collage representing another member of the group.

To Play:

The name of each person in the group is written on a slip of paper, so that everyone can draw someone else's name. When the names have been drawn, each participant looks through magazines for pictures that remind him of positive qualities of the person's name he drew. He then cuts out the pictures and pastes them on a piece of construction paper to form a collage. When the collages are complete, the others may try to guess which person is represented by each collage. The artists then explain their creations. The subjects of the collages may wish to take them home as reminders of how they are appreciated by others.

A Different Door Prize

Number of Players: 8–100

Length of Time: 10–15 minutes

Materials: Numbers are written on slips of paper to be drawn from a hat. The same numbers are written on name tags as people arrive, or are simply distributed to those present.

Object of the Game: To help players feel more comfortable with showing affection.

To Play:

During a party or other gathering, numbers are drawn from a hat for a door prize. When the winners have been announced, the prize is revealed: the love of the brethren. All the others present then convey their brotherly love to the winners by means of hugs, words of encouragement, and other acceptable expressions of affection. The winners really do feel special.

Symbolic Gifts

Number of Players: 4–10

Length of Time: 30 minutes to 2 hours

Object of the Game: To give symbolic gifts of love.

To Play:

A period of time is provided for everyone to search the meeting place for an appropriate gift to give each of the others in the group. The gifts need not be valuable in themselves, but instead are symbolic. The givers should consider what they want to communicate to each of the others. For instance, a light bulb might be given someone with a radiant personality, or a cookbook to someone who is hungry for the Lord. The gifts can be very creative, and can be objects that will need to be returned, since they are intended as symbols, not necessarily for use. However, to be meaningful, they should be positive, rather than humorous in a negative way. When the gifts are all collected, each member of the group presents his gifts, explaining the meaning behind each one.

ACTIVE GAMES

At last! Here are ways to exercise, race, even play ball, without producing losers.

See Also:

Nonelimination Musical Chairs
Feather Blow
Caterpillar Over the Mountain
Games for School-Age Children
People-to-People
Barrel of Monkeys
Machine Charades
Continuous Story
Chock Chiddle Po Po
Musical Poses
Water Games
T-Shirt Tower

People Express

Number of Players: 3–30

Length of Time: 5–30 minutes

Materials: Objects with which to create obstacles

Preparation: Objects are arranged to serve as obstacles.

Object of Game: To keep the "train" connected as it moves through the obstacle course.

To Play:

Players form a line, each holding the waist of the person in front of him. The person at the front of the line leads the train quickly through the obstacle course. The other players follow, keeping the train together. Players may take turns being the leader, rearranging the obstacles or taking a different route each time.

Variations:

1. All players except the leader are blindfolded.
2. Players try to complete the course without laughing.

Push'em into Balance

Number of Players: Any even number

Length of Time: 2–15 minutes

Object of Game: For partners to push each other to in-
                          dependent standing positions.

To Play:

The group pairs off, and the players in each twosome lean toward each other hand-to-hand, so that they are dependent on each other to keep from falling. Then they attempt to push each other into independent standing positions without moving their feet.

Variations:

1. Players kneel hand-to-hand, inch farther and farther apart, then push each other back to kneeling position.
2. Players kneel, then push each other up to stand on their feet.
3. Players sit on the floor, back-to-back, and push each other up to a semi-standing position. They then roll against each other until they stand facing each other, leaning into each other's hands, and play "Push'em into Balance" as in *To Play* above.
4. Any of the above versions might be played on a bench, balance beam, or other apparatus.
5. Three or more players compose a partnership instead of two.

Log Roll

Number of Players: 7–20

Length of Time: 10–30 minutes

Object of the Game: To get a rolling ride on living logs.

To Play:

All players except one lie face down, side by side. The remaining player lies face down on the backs of the other players, perpendicular to them. The players on the bottom then roll over slowly, all in the same direction. They continue rolling until their passenger is propelled to the floor at the end opposite where he started. The passenger then lies with the other "log" players at the end of the line, and the log at the beginning of the line becomes a passenger. The game continues until all the logs have had at least one turn at being a passenger.

Variation:

If some of the players are light enough, they can ride double-file over the logs.

Comment:

Larger players may need to support some of their own weight as they ride.

Skin the Snake

Number of Players: 5–50

Length of Time: 10–20 minutes

Object of the Game: To lie down and stand up without breaking the chain.

To Play:

The players form a line and bend forward slightly. Each player puts his right hand through his legs and uses his left hand to grasp the right hand of the person in front of him. The last person in line lies down (carefully), while the other players walk backward, straddling him. Each player lies down when he gets to the end. During this process all players must continue holding hands. If the chain is broken, they must start over. When all players are lying down, the last person to lie down gets up and walks forward reversing the procedure, until all are standing again. The players may then challenge themselves to skin the snake faster and more efficiently. For a very large group, however, getting everyone down and up again is enough of an accomplishment.

Crack the Whip

Number of Players: 5–20

Length of Time: 10–30 minutes

Playing Site: Safe ground for falling

Object of the Game: To produce a thrilling run for the end
                          of the "whip."

To Play:

The players hold hands in a line. They may wish to alternate
the directions they are facing. The person at the head of the
line starts running, pulling the rest of the "whip" after him.
The more he changes direction as he runs, the more fun it
will be for those at the other end of the whip (and the more
difficult it will be not to break off and fall to the ground!). The
players should rotate positions periodically to give everyone
a turn at both ends of the "whip."

Variation:

"Crack the Whip" can be played on skates.

Race to a Tie

Number of Players: 2–20

Length of Time: 5–20 minutes

Playing Site: Indoor track or outdoors

Preparation: Starting and finishing lines are established.

Object of the Game: For all participants to cross the finish line at the same moment.

To Play:

The players line up at the starting line, and run to the finishing line, keeping an eye on each other, so that they all cross the finishing line at the same time. If players wish to improve their synchronization they can repeat the race as many times as necessary.

Variations:

1. The race can be done swimming, cycling, walking backward, etc., for added challenge and amusement.
2. Players follow different routes to the same goal. Routes can be charted through various obstacles.

Comment:

Racing to a tie is more difficult than it sounds, particularly with a large number of players and a variety of ages.

Tell Your Time

Number of Players: 1–100

Length of Time: 5–20 minutes

Materials: Clock or watch with a second hand

Playing Site: Indoor track or outdoors

Preparation: Starting and finishing lines are established.

Object of the Game: To correctly estimate the time it takes to run a given distance.

To Play:

The players each estimate how long it will take them to run the distance indicated, and after running it, find out how close their respective estimates were. They can do this by means of a clock visible from the starting and finishing lines, or by one or more timekeepers who call out the times as players cross the finish line. If the run is repeated, players can try to improve on their previous estimates.

Variations:

Other means of travel, such as walking, skipping, swimming or cycling can be employed.

Comment:

The players "race" but focus on their own skill at estimation rather than on comparing their speed with that of other runners.

Relay Against the Clock

Number of Players: 4–100

Length of Time: 10–30 minutes

Materials: Stopwatch or any watch with a second hand; other materials, depending on the relay

Preparation: Varies according to relay.

Object of the Game: To improve on the time it takes to complete the relay.

To Play:

Any relay race can be converted to a contest against the clock instead of against other teams. (Variations are given below.) If the group is small enough, players all work at the same task. The task is repeated as many times as desired, attempting with each try to shorten the time it takes to complete it. Larger groups can be divided into squads, each at a different station. The times of all of them are added together, and the whole group tries to shorten their total time the next round.

Variations:

1. A water bucket is emptied by each player taking a turn at scooping out a cupful.
2. Players race, one by one, to a designated point and back, running, hopping, walking backward, balancing a book on the head, kicking a balloon, running in a potato sack, or whatever you can dream up. They stop when all players have completed the course.
3. A ball is passed down the line of players alternately between the legs and over the head. The last person runs to

the front of the line and continues passing. The task is completed when the original first person is again at the front of the line.

Long, Long, Long Jump

Number of Players: 3–12

Length of Time: 10–30 minutes

Material: Measuring tape

Playing Site: Gymnasium or outdoors

Object of the Game: To achieve the longest possible jump.

To Play:

Each player in turn tries to jump as far as possible, beginning his jump where the previous player left off. When all have jumped, the total distance is measured. Players then repeat the process, trying to improve the total distance jumped.

Variations:

1. Any kind of a jump can be used: standing, running or backward broadjump, one-legged or two-legged, with two players holding hands, etc.
2. A different style of jumping is used with each round, to compare the total distance achieved by each style.
3. A ball or Frisbee is thrown by each player. Each player throws the ball from the spot where the previous player landed it.
4. Each player runs (or skips, hops, etc.) as far as possible during a very short timed period. The next player begins where the previous player stopped.

Bat the Bat

Number of Players: 2–12

Length of Time: 20–90 minutes

Materials: Softball, bat, gloves

Playing Site: Large paved area or field (the flatter the better)

Object of the Game: To hit the bat with the ball.

To Play:

A batter throws the ball up and hits it into the field, where the other players are waiting to catch it. The batter then places his bat on the ground in front of him. The player who catches the ball or retrieves it from the ground then throws or rolls the ball, trying to strike the bat without moving from the spot where the ball fell. If the fielder succeeds in striking the bat, he trades places with the batter. Otherwise, the batter takes another turn.

In and Out

Number of Players: 10–30

Length of Time: 10–45 minutes

Materials: Beach ball or rubber ball

Playing Site: Large room or outside

Object of the Game: To get or remain in the middle of the circle.

To Play:

The players are divided into two groups: those who stand in the form of a circle and those who stand in the middle of the circle. The players in the circumference of the circle take turns throwing the ball at players in the middle. When a player in the middle is hit with the ball, the player who threw the ball exchanges places with him. The game can continue this way indefinitely.

Variations:

1. To increase team work: The ball must be passed one or more times among the circle players before it can be thrown at a middle player.
2. With a large group, a wide-spaced circle of players is stationed inside the main circle. This makes it more difficult to hit moving players. Inner circle players should be rotated regularly.

Comment:

"In and Out" does involve a competitive element, but since players are constantly moving in and out, there are no real winners or losers.

Pin

Number of Players: 1–12

Length of Time: 10–60 minutes

Materials: 2 or more balls, a bowling pin or sim-
                           ilar object

Playing Site: Large room or outdoors

Object of the Game: To make the lead ball touch the pin
                           without knocking it over.

To Play:

A pin is placed on the floor at a reasonable distance from the players, who stand in a line, all facing the pin. The first player rolls the lead ball toward the pin, trying to get the ball close to the pin without knocking it over. The second player rolls his ball toward the lead ball, so as to move the lead ball closer to the pin. Ideally, each player has his own ball which he in turn rolls to push the lead ball closer to the pin, until the lead ball is touching the standing pin. If fewer balls are available, balls that have already been rolled can be retrieved for use by other players. However, the lead ball must not be moved except by the other balls. When the lead ball is touching the standing pin, the players have won the game. If the pin is knocked over, the player who knocked it down rolls the lead ball to begin a new game.

Variations:

1. The players form two lines, on opposite sides of the pin. This way, if the lead ball is rolled *past* the pin, the players on the other side of the pin can push it back.

Ball Games

2. Instead of standing in a straight line, players stand in a
    circle around the pin.

Comment:

"Pin" originated with the Guatemalan Indians.

Square Ball

Number of Players: 12–24

Length of Time: 10–60 minutes

Materials: For every four players: a ball, a 12–16 foot rope, and a base

Playing Site: Large room or outdoors

Preparation: The bases are spaced equidistantly in a large circle.

Object of the Game: To pass the balls completely around the circle.

To Play:

Four players are stationed at each base, with a rope and a ball. Each group holds the rope taut in the shape of a square, with each player at a corner, and the ball on the floor within the bounds of the square. Each group transports its ball to the next counter-clockwise base by passing it from foot to foot within the confines of the rope, which the players continue to hold taut. The team members must then hurry back to their original base, still in the shape of a square, to repeat the procedure with the ball that the team behind them has left them. The game continues until each team has its original ball back.

Variations:

1. For an additional challenge, the players try to make the circuit within a certain time limit.
2. If more confusion is desired, additional balls may be introduced.

Ball Games

Comment:

If the balls are different in appearance, it will be easier for the teams to know when they have their original balls back.

Blowball

Number of Players:	5–20
Length of Time:	10–30 minutes
Materials:	One or more Ping-Pong balls
Playing Site:	Large, smooth floor area or table; a rug or blanket sling (for variation)
Preparation:	Parallel lines are established across which the ball(s) must be blown.
Object of the Game:	To blow one or more Ping-Pong balls across a line or lines as many times as possible in a given time period.

To Play:

Two lines of players face each other, either lying prone on the floor, or standing on opposite sides of a table. Two parallel lines lie between them, with the Ping-Pong ball(s) between the lines. The players blow the ball(s) back and forth from line to line as many times as possible in a given time period, scoring a point each time the ball crosses a line. They can repeat the game as many times as desired, attempting to improve their score.

Variations:

1. One player lies sideways on a rug or blanket, with his head hanging over the side. He blows the ball from line to line, while other players carry or drag the sling to keep him close to the ball, turning him around when he needs to blow it the other direction. Each player takes a turn in the sling as the group tries to improve its score.

Ball Games

2. Each player is carried in a sling, blowing from one line to the next, for only one trip. The players try to improve the time it takes to make each trip.

Comment:

With a large group, having several balls in play will maximize participation.

Long Volley

Number of Players: 4–20

Length of Time: 15–60 minutes

Material: Volleyball

Playing Site: Gym or playing field

Object of the Game: To volley the ball to the end of the field
                          without letting it fall.

To Play:

A player begins the game by serving the ball toward the other
players. All the players then work together to advance the ball
to an appointed goal at one end of the field or gym, passing
the ball in volleyball fashion. If the ball drops to the ground,
they must start over. Once they are confident with the game,
the team members may wish to add the following variations
to the rules.

Variations:

1. Players attempt to advance the ball with as few passes as
    possible.
2. Players attempt to advance the ball with as many passes
    as possible.
3. All players must touch the ball before a goal can be scored.
4. Two balls are in play at once, going the same or opposite
    directions.

Comments:

"Long Volley" varies considerably in intensity, depending on the number of players and the size of the field. If only 4 persons are playing, they will all get quite a workout. If 20 are playing, some of the variations above may be needed to make sure everyone participates.

Perpetual Volley

Number of Players: 6–20

Length of Time: 5–60 minutes

Materials: Volleyball and net

Object of the Game: To volley the ball as many successive
                          times as possible without letting it fall.

To Play:

The players are arranged in equal teams on either side of the
net. A player serves the volleyball or simply tosses it into play.
Both teams have the same simple goal: to keep the ball in
play. They count the number of times the ball is tapped before
it inevitably falls to the ground, then play a new game, attempting to improve the old score. The following variations
can be applied separately or in combination.

Variations:

1. The ball must not be touched twice in a row by the same
   player.
2. The ball can be touched only once (or alternatively, twice
   or three times) on each side of the net before it goes over.
3. The ball must be touched by three different players before
   it crosses the net.
4. The ball must be passed to every player on the team before
   it crosses the net.
5. Instead of counting hits, the players keep the ball in play
   for as long a *time* as possible.
6. The group times how long it takes for the ball to be touched
   by all the players. The group then tries to reduce its time.
7. Children may catch the ball and throw it instead of just
   tapping it.

Ball Games

8. The net is covered with a blanket to increase the suspense.
9. Tennis or badminton equipment is used instead of volleyball.

All on One Side

Number of Players: 4–9

Length of Time: 10–30 minutes

Materials: Balloon(s) and a volleyball net

Object of the Game: To get all the players to the other side
                           of the net.

To Play:

All the players stand on one side of the net and pass the balloon among themselves in volleyball fashion. After each player taps the balloon, he scurries under the net and waits for the others to join him. The last player to receive the balloon volleys it over the net before he joins the others to begin the game again. The team tries to change sides as many times as possible without letting the balloon touch the floor.

Variation:

Two balloons are used at once.

Blanketball

Number of Players: 8–24

Length of Time: 10–60 minutes

Materials: Two large blankets and one or two beach balls

Playing Site: Large room with a high ceiling or outdoors

Object of the Game: To pass the ball from blanket to blanket.

To Play:

The group is divided into two teams. The members of each team space themselves around a blanket, holding the edges. One team places the beach ball on its blanket. After rolling and tossing the ball for a while to get used to the feel of it, they propel the ball to the other team. The other team catches the ball and returns it in like manner. As their skill develops, players can further challenge themselves by increasing the distance between the blankets or by trying the variations below.

Variations:

1. The serving team tosses the ball straight up, then runs out from under it so the receiving team can catch it.
2. Each team is given a ball to be exchanged simultaneously with the other team.
3. Two or more balls are juggled by a single team or between two teams.
4. The ball is propelled over a volleyball net. The teams try to volley it as many times as possible before they drop the ball.

5. A rubber ball or soccer ball is used instead of a beach ball.
    The heavier ball will make longer passes possible.

Comment:

"Blanketball" fosters teamwork because playing is impossible
without everyone's cooperation.

WATER GAMES

Water provides an excellent setting for trying new capers, because falling doesn't hurt. That can be important for those attempting "Inner Tube Balance"! The players' imaginations should lead them to create other swimming site games.

See Also:

Race to a Tie
Tell Your Time
High Water

Water Pass

Number of Players: 8–30

Length of Time: 5–20 minutes

Materials: Ball or other object, clock

Object of the Game: To pass the ball around the circle as quickly as possible.

To Play:

Players stand in a circle in the water and pass a ball all the way around. Since the objective is to complete the circuit as quickly as possible, a clock may be watched to see if the group's time is improved with successive attempts, or a buzzer may be sounded after a certain time has elapsed. If the ball is dropped, the player who lost it must swim or dive to retrieve the ball and put it back in play.

Variation:

Other objects may be substituted for the ball to make the game more challenging. Try a greased watermelon, for instance.

Water Bridge

Number of Players: 9–20

Length of Time: 10–40 minutes

Object of the Game: To get a player across the pool without
                           getting him wet.

To Play:

All players but one stand double file in the pool, each person
linking wrists with the player across from him. The other
person crosses the pool by crawling across the bridge they
have thus formed. Depending on the number of players, it
may be necessary for the players at the beginning of the bridge
to run to the end of the bridge to continue the structure,
after the crosser has passed them. Each person takes a turn
crossing the bridge.

Variations:

1. Instead of standing passively, the players in the pool pass
    the crosser to other players or to inner tubes.
2. If the bridge is long enough, more than one player may
    cross at a time.

Comment:

The waterbound players should understand that it is their
responsibility to keep the crosser dry, not wet.

Log Chute

Number of Players: 10–20

Length of Time: 10–30 minutes

Object of the Game: To create a water current on which to ride.

To Play:

The players stand in two lines facing each other, each person joining hands with the player he is facing. They create a current by moving their hands in a circle just under the water's surface, all in the same direction. This turns the area between the two lines into a water chute. The two players at the source of the current ride down the chute one at a time, floating on their backs. When they reach the mouth of the chute, they rejoin hands to continue the current. The next two players take a turn, until all have had a ride.

Inner Tube Balance

Number of Players: 4 or groups of 4

Length of Time: 5–20 minutes

Materials: A large inner tube for every four players

Object of the Game: For all four players to be standing on the inner tube at the same time.

To Play:

As the inner tube floats on the water, the players climb onto it. They help each other to a standing position so that all four are standing on the tube at once.

Variations:

1. Players maintain the standing position as long as possible.
2. Smaller groups (2 or 3) stand on smaller inner tubes.
3. Players can use their imaginations for other balancing tricks.

STUNTS

These games use ordinary objects in extraordinary ways. Young people will especially enjoy trying them.

See Also:

> *Sock-Off*
> *Barrel of Monkeys*
> *Greasy Spoon*
> *Interdependence*
> *Inner Tube Balance*

Fifty-Two Put-Down

Number of Players: 4–20

Length of Time: 10–20 minutes

Materials: Deck of cards, clock

Object of the Game: To play the deck as quickly as possible.

To Play:

A deck of cards is distributed to a group seated in a circle. Whoever has the two of diamonds places it in the center, face up. The person with the three of diamonds quickly does the same, and so on through the suit. When the diamonds have all been played, the group goes on to hearts, then clubs, then spades. Since the object is to play the whole deck as quickly as possible, the group may wish to time itself and try to improve by playing again.

Variation:

Two decks are used, and each suit is run twice. This version will compound the confusion because two players will be holding each card.

Gift-Wrap Grapple

Number of Players: 2–20

Length of Time: 10–20 minutes

Materials: Boxes and gift-wrapping parapher-
                          nalia

Object of the Game: To wrap a gift as a team.

To Play:

The group is divided into teams of two. Each team is given a
box to wrap, and gift-wrapping materials are made available
to all. The task of each team is to wrap a "gift" with each
person using only one hand. One member of the team keeps
his left hand behind his back, and the other member his
right hand. Thus, they try to function as one person with a
right and left hand.

Variation:

For added challenge, a limited amount of time is allowed in
which to wrap the gifts.

Comment:

"Gift-Wrap Grapple" is a good cooperation exercise that will
also produce some laughs.

T-Shirt Tower

Number of Players: 10–20

Length of Time: 5–20 minutes

Material: One (old) T-shirt

Object of the Game: To fit as many people as possible on the tower.

To Play:

The group tries to fit as many of its members as possible on/ over a T-shirt without any touching the floor. The last known record is 11.

High Water

Number of Players: 2–20

Length of Time: 5–30 minutes

Materials: Tub, oilcloth or sheet of plastic, measuring cup, pitcher, chair

Preparation: The measuring cup is placed in the tub on top of the waterproof cloth. The chair is placed next to the tub, and a pitcher of water is close at hand.

Playing Site: Outdoors or a room that will not be damaged by water.

Object of the Game: To pour as much water as possible into the measuring cup.

To Play:

Each player, one at a time, mounts the chair, and holding the pitcher of water above his shoulders, tries to pour as much water as possible into the measuring cup. The participants should focus on encouraging their fellow players rather than on surpassing them. When everyone has had a turn, players may try another round to improve their techniques.

Chuckle Chain

Number of Players: 6–20

Length of Time: 10–30 minutes

Object of the Game: To have a good chuckle.

To Play:

The first player lies with his back on the floor. The second player lies perpendicular to the first player, with his head on the first player's abdomen. The other players recline similarly, making a zigzag chain across the floor. The first player then begins the chuckle chain by saying "Ha." The second player follows with, "Ha, ha," the third with, "Ha, ha, ha," and so on. If the players can do this successfully—their heads will be bouncing every time their headrests breathe—they may go on to more complicated chuckle chains in follow-the-leader fashion.

Comment:

"Chuckle Chain" is a good means of loosening up a group. In fact, it may be impossible to complete the game without being interrupted by waves of spontaneous chuckles.

TRAVEL GAMES

Appropriate for a wide range of ages, for families, youth groups, or anyone traveling by car or bus, these are games that keep a carfull busy for hours.

See Also:

Circle and Pass-It-On Games
Daffy Definitions
Finish the Mystery
Word Games
Headlines
Rhythm and Music Games
Storytelling Games
Reminiscing
Forgiveness Exercise

How Far?

Number of Players: 3–10

Length of Time: 5–20 minutes

Materials: Clock or watch

Object of the Game: To guess how far the car has traveled
                          in a brief period of time.

To Play:

The passengers all close their eyes and try to guess when the
car has traveled a mile. When a player thinks a mile has been
traveled, he opens his eyes and checks the odometer, remaining silent until all the other players have done the same.
The players may repeat the game and attempt to improve
their estimates, or try to estimate greater distances.

Variations:

1. The players close their eyes until the driver tells them to
   open them, then all guess how far they have traveled during the time period.
2. The players keep their eyes open.

Map Quiz

Number of Players: 2–10

Length of Time: 5 minutes to 2 hours

Materials: Road map or atlas

Object of the Game: To answer geography questions correctly.

To Play:

The leader, who holds the map, poses questions to the other players and compares their answers with the information found on the map. These questions may take various forms:

1. If a U.S. map is available, the leader names a state and says, "North." The other players try to correctly identify the state(s) north of the one named. The leader may then continue by saying, "south," "east," and "west." If a world atlas is available, he may name countries in the same manner.

2. The leader names a highway. The others try to name the cities or states, in order, if possible, that the highway traverses.

3. The leader names various cities (if the players are traveling, he can name the ones they will be passing on their way), and the others give their estimates as to the population of each. If the population is not posted on the highway, the leader might wait until they are through the city before giving the answer, allowing the others to observe the city itself for clues before giving their final bids.

4. The leader names two cities, asking the others to estimate the distance between them.

5. The leader asks the others to identify the states that various national parks are in.

6. Many other questions may be posed, depending on the map and the players' imaginations.

Highway Alphabet

Number of Players: 1–10

Length of Time: 20 minutes to 2 hours or more

Object of the Game: To spot all the letters of the alphabet.

To Play:

The travelers must observe all the letters of the alphabet, in order, on whatever road signs or license plates they encounter. Whenever someone sees the letter they are looking for, he calls it out, so that the group will know what to look for next.

Variations:

1. When the alphabet is complete, players look for "Ab," "Ac," "Ad," etc.
2. The initial letters of the books of the Bible, in order, must be identified: first, "G" for Genesis, then "E" for Exodus, etc.
3. Numbers are identified instead of letters, starting with one and going as high as possible.
4. Each letter or number must be found on a different sign.
5. Only license plates or only billboards are used.
6. Several variations may be played simultaneously by individuals or small teams within a car.

License-Plate Logo

Number of Players: 1–6

Length of Time: Indefinite

Preparation: The best time to play is during the day.

Object of the Game: To make words from the license plates of other cars.

To Play:

When someone spots a license plate, he reads the letters aloud. Everyone then tries to think of words with those letters in them in the same order as they appear on the license plate. For instance, the letters "LRD" might generate the words, "lurid," "learned," and "colored." Players call out the words as they come to mind.

Comment:

"License-Plate Logo" is appropriately challenging to a wide range of abilities, since some letter combinations are easy, and some very difficult. It can be enjoyed during a short ride to town, or while driving across a continent!

License-Plate Lexicon

Number of Players: 1–10

Length of Time: 5 minutes to several hours

Object of the Game: To think of Bible subjects suggested by license plates.

To Play:

For each license plate observed, the travelers must think of Bible subjects (characters, places, etc.) that start with the letters on it. "BCM" might suggest "Benjamin," "Christ" and "Mount Zion." The variations below are ways to make the game more challenging.

Variations:

1. The first license plate must be associated with Bible characters, the next one with places, the next one with objects; or animals, Old Testament figures, New Testament figures, etc., may be used.
2. The first license-plate letter can be used for any Bible subject, but the other letters must be related to the first subject named. For instance, if the letters are "FAD" and "F" suggests "frankincense," then "A" and "D" should also be associated with the wise men or the nativity. "A" might become "Augustus"—the emperor whose decree brought Mary and Joseph to Bethlehem; and "D" might be for "donkey," Mary's mode of travel.
3. Players may refer to their Bibles if necessary.
4. Other themes besides the Bible are used.

Pedidel

Number of Players: 2–6

Length of Time: 20–90 minutes

Preparation: "Pedidel" must be played at night.

Object of Game: To spot as many cars as possible with only one headlight.

To Play:

During a fixed period of time, the group tries to spot cars with only one working headlight. When a player sees such a car, he says, "Pedidel" (pronounced pe-di´del). A count of pedidels is kept to accumulate as many as possible during the set period of time.

Variations:

1. In addition to watching for pedidels, the group must also watch for ledideps ("ledidep" is "pedidel" spelled backward), which are cars with burned-out taillights. For each ledidep, one is subtracted from the count of pedidels.
2. During the day other vehicles can be counted and added or subtracted, such as trucks, trailers, Volkswagons, etc.

Bible-Subject Search

Number Players: 2–10

Length of Time: 5 minutes to several hours

Object of the Game: To find subjects found in the Bible.

To Play:

Players observe the area traveled and try to identify as many objects as possible that are mentioned in the Bible. These might include sheep, clouds, farmers, thorns, etc. Players might increase their knowledge by reading their Bibles as they go, to get ideas for what to look for.

Variation:

If two or more cars are traveling the same road, the passengers can compare their findings at the end of the trip or at a stop along the way.

Travel Treasure Hunt

Number of Players: 2–10

Length of Time: 15 minutes to several hours

Preparation: The group prepares a list of objects they will look for on their trip. The objects may vary as to their likelihood of being spotted. Examples: a tractor in operation, a tow truck, a spotted horse, a red car with a blue license plate, a car made more than 20 years ago, etc.

Object of the Game: To identify objects on the list.

To Play:

The group works together to locate and check off objects from the list as they travel.

Motorcar Medley

Number of Players: 1–10

Length of Time: 5–30 minutes

Preparation: "Motorcar Medley" must be played while traveling a road with intermittent intersections.

Object of the Game: To change songs at each intersection.

To Play:

Any songs may be used for this game, but the players may wish to choose a theme such as hymns, camp songs, or show tunes. The travelers begin singing a song, but whenever they cross an intersection, they must start singing a new song. The new song can be started by an appointed song-leader, or the players take turns starting new songs, or the choice of song can be left to whoever thinks of one first.

Variation:

On a moderately bumpy road, each bump signals a change of song.

ALPHABETICAL INDEX

TOPICAL INDEX

CHILDREN

CIRCLE GAMES

COMMUNICATION GAMES

CONCENTRATION GAMES

WATER GAMES

WORD GAMES